PROSPER ON PURPOSE

Melody Thompson

Copyright © 2018 Melody Thompson.

All rights reserved. No part of this publication may be reproduced, distributed or transmitted in any form or by any means, including photocopying, recording, or other electronic or mechanical methods, without the prior written permission of the publisher, except in the case of brief quotations embodied in critical reviews and certain other noncommercial uses permitted by copyright law.

Prosper on Purpose | Melody Thompson -- 1st edition

ISBN-13: 978-1-7324270-0-6

Table of Contents

INTRO - PROSPER ON PURPOSE 1
Prosperity and Purpose 2

CHAPTER 1 - PERSONALITY 7
Your Identity 7
Authenticity 16
Gifts 30
Intelligence 34
Strengths 41

CHAPTER 2 – PERSPECTIVE 53
What Is Mindset? 61
Dealing with Critics 66
Changing Your Mindset and Getting Unstuck 70
Taking Accountability for Our Lives 80
Negative Internal Promises™ (NIPs™) 88

CHAPTER 3 – PASSION 91
What is Passion? 91
Values 98
Your Legacy 105

CHAPTER 4 - POSITION 107

Your Internal GPS 107

Your Position in Life 108

Play Your Position 113

Vision and Goals 116

Motivations and Aspirations 117

CHAPTER 5 – POWER 127

The Importance of Power 128

Creating Healthy Boundaries 138

Developing an Empowered Mindset 144

ARISE Method™ for Empowerment 146

Personal Power 152

Lifestyle Modifications 169

CHAPTER 6 – PURPOSE 175

Passion vs. Purpose 175

Myths About Purpose 177

Types of Purpose 180

The Phases of Purpose™ 181

Defining Your Purpose 190

CONCLUSION 207

INTRO - PROSPER ON PURPOSE

Many people believe prosperity is all about money and material possessions. While money and material things are associated with prosperity, they don't represent the whole picture. You're probably used to thinking of money as a tangible object that resides in your wallet or sits in your bank account until you're ready to use it. You pay bills with it, purchase products and services with it and maybe even donate some of it to worthwhile charities. If you're like most people, you probably have a job or business through which you exchange time, products or services for money.

Prosperity can be described as success, health, wealth and wholeness in every area of your life. Prosperity can also be described as the ability to flourish in your mind, body, spirit, relationships, career and life. It includes having love, joy and peace. When you have wholeness within yourself, it will ultimately allow you to attain and maintain the wonderful things life has to offer. It is important to know your joy is your strength, your peace is your prosperity and your wealth is within.

Many people focus on success as an outward accomplishment they must achieve. The truth is real success is built from the inside out. Success often reveals and magnifies who we already are on the inside.

We must focus on who we are internally, rather than focusing so intently on achieving accolades, accomplishments and applause alone. On our journey to success, who we become in the process is more important than what we achieve. Overcoming the challenges, obstacles and setbacks on our journey help to shape our character. Success is more about working on our *being,* rather than focusing solely on what we are doing. External things are temporary, they come and go. Who we are on the inside is what really matters.

You don't want to be in pursuit of success and lose the most important things around you, including yourself. Prosperity is about having balance in all areas, so that you are not a public success and a private mess. Some people are so concerned about gaining success that they are willing to attain it by any means necessary. True prosperity comes from operating in honesty and integrity without compromising our morals and values in order to achieve success.

Prosperity and Purpose

Many times I find people pursue a career and even start a business with a desire to make money. When we have this mindset, it is often difficult to prosper because the desire is focused on what *we* want and how *we* want it to be. When we pursue a career or a business without contemplating our purpose, it is hard for it to sustain itself because it's only purpose is to make money. If you are not aware of your passion, talents, gifts, or motivation for what you do, over time it will be difficult to sustain momentum. Your success is attached to your level of passion and purpose.

All true success and prosperity must be attached to knowing who you are, what you are here to do and how your purpose helps others. As we will learn later in this book, our purpose is always greater than ourselves and it always involves helping others. I also believe it must be in line with our gifts, talents and skill sets. We must also understand our success and prosperity is not for our benefit alone, but to help others.

Success without purpose can result in wasting our money, time and talents in the wrong places. Knowing our purpose is what helps us to move in the right direction and become intentional, passionate and motivated about what we do. Finding purpose is a journey on the pathway of life. Our purpose is the vehicle we use to reach our destiny. Our passion is the fuel that keeps us going.

I have found that life rarely turns out the way we want it to be. I believe the cause of this is because we don't surrender to what *should* be. If we live our lives always trying to make something happen the way we *want* it to be, we could miss out on the life we are supposed to live. The life we are supposed to live is always much greater than what we had in mind.

Many people believe that we are in total control of our lives and our destinies. I believe our destiny is already written before we are ever born. I believe sometimes people don't reach their destiny because they may be determined to have it their way and never get what was *pre-destined* for them. Some people meet the wrong people and make the wrong choices. Many settle for less because it seemed best to them. Some never had a fair chance to begin with. While we do have control over our actions, I have also realized there is much out of our control in this life. This is why surrendering and coming into alignment with our purpose is so important.

Prosperity and Health

Prospering in our health is not just about physical health. Sometimes there are emotional connections to physical diseases. Sometimes we have to deal with our own emotional issues so we can truly have success in our lives.

When you are healed and whole within, you will prosper in your physical health, emotional health and in your life. It is difficult to prosper when you are broken inside. If you are broken inside, somewhere in your life something else is broke, broken, broke down or breaking down. When you are whole, everything else in your life can flourish and prosper. When some area of your life is broken, it affects your whole life. I want you to prosper and be healthy, wealthy, wise *and* whole. You don't have to be perfect, but you can be whole.

Most people have their hearts broken somewhere in their lives, but they never take the time to heal from it. Maybe it was from a traumatic relationship, a job, a failed business, a marriage, a death, a disappointment, abandonment, sickness, failure, abuse, etc. Most people just patch their pain with a temporary band-aid and keep going, simply because they have to. It is not acceptable in our society to say we are hurting inside, so most people never tell anyone. They suffer in silence, until everything starts to fall apart and they can't hide it anymore.

Some people are great at masking their issues so no one knows; others are more obvious with their pain. Whatever your issue, the most important thing to do is take the time to heal your issues. I tell people, "Deal so you can heal." You have to deal with the issues of your heart, because out of your heart flows all the issues of your life. You have to heal your heart, so you can flow in abundance, prosperity and purpose. If you don't fix your issues, you will find yourself in a place of lack continually, without understanding why you can't seem to get ahead.

It's Your Time to Prosper on Purpose

I want you to win but the way you are going to win is not by settling, copying others, compromising your integrity, hiding in fear or waiting for someone to give you permission. You are going to win by tapping into your identity, finding your purpose and living out your destiny. It's time for you to live your dreams. It's time for you to pick your dream up off the shelf

PROSPER ON PURPOSE

and dust it off. If you tried it before and it didn't work, I'm here to tell you – try it again.

Maybe you were ahead of your time, it happens, especially to visionaries. Who knows, the product that didn't work ten years ago, may be the product everyone wants today. Maybe you weren't ready to handle the success then, or maybe you didn't have enough experience. Maybe others sabotaged your success or maybe you experienced unexpected circumstances. Perhaps you've never fully pursued your dream with all your heart. Maybe you only dipped your toes into the waters and didn't fully commit to it. Well, now is the time to dive in, however this time you will do it differently.

Your situation may not have turned out the way you wanted, but it did happen, whether you liked it or not. Now, instead of continuing to mourn what was lost, let's ask, what fortunes can you find in your failures? What lessons can you learn? It's time for you to be intentional about your life and make the decision to prosper on purpose.

This book is founded on the principle that personal success and fulfillment ultimately come from a keen sense of identity and purpose. Throughout this book you will be guided through a self discovery process, which covers essential personal development components including: identity, vision, values, beliefs, goals, skills, power and success.

I wrote this book to help individuals discover their identity, purpose and personal power in order to be prosperous in life and in the marketplace. I have created a six step framework that takes a comprehensive look at the whole person, which will result in discovering the gateway to your purpose. We will discuss the six areas and what part they play in your journey of self-discovery. I want you to live an abundant life. It is possible for you to know your purpose and live in your greatness, so ultimately you can go change the world. Now is the time. Are you ready?

CHAPTER 1 - PERSONALITY

Your personality and identity are the foundations of self discovery and the starting point of your purpose and everything else about you. Your personality and identity are unique. There are over seven billion people on the planet, however there is no one like you in the world currently and no one like you will ever exist again in the future. Your individuality is evidenced by your unique fingerprint, which no one else possesses. Knowing your identity will keep you grounded as you journey through life to discover your purpose.

Your Identity

There are some misconceptions about what makes up a person's identity. Many people understand their identity to be what they have, what they do or who they are in relation to others. People even believe they are who others say they are. However, none of these make up your true identity, because any one of those factors can change at any moment, which would leave you on a search to find your identity again. The identity discovery process is like peeling away the layers of an onion, until you get to your true authentic self.

No matter what your circumstances are at this present moment, just know you are rich. You are rich in wisdom, rich in experiences, rich in accomplishments, rich in gifts and talents, rich in knowledge.

Even if you think you have nothing left to give or if you think you have failed in the past, you are better now than you have ever been before. Even if you haven't made the best choices in the past, as of today, you may be rich in knowing what *not* to do, rich in knowing what *doesn't* work for you and rich in knowing who *isn't* for you. That's wisdom! No matter the outcome, no one can ever take away the richness of your experiences.

"Ordinary riches can be stolen, real riches cannot.

In your soul are infinitely precious things that cannot be taken from you."

-Oscar Wilde

While these experiences don't define us, they do help in some way to shape who we will become. You simply have to learn to find the gold nuggets in all of your experiences – the good experiences, the bad experiences and even the ugly ones. There are gold nuggets to be found in all of the experiences in your life and throughout this book we are going to deep dive into the depths of your soul to find them. By the end of this book, you will discover the richness of who you are, and how you can use it to help others and change the world around you.

What Makes Up Your Identity?

Just to clear up some myths about identity: You are not defined by your occupation, material possessions, income, education, socioeconomic status, environment or associations. These are used by society to define and measure success and relevance. All of these things are external factors and cannot completely define you. The only things that can truly define you are within you.

We must learn to separate ourselves from external factors, in order to focus on our true identity within. The processes of self reflection and self discovery are so important, because they allow you to discover who you *really* are within, without outside influences.

Some of the factors that determine one's identity are:

- Genetics
- Family History
- Your Name
- Your Personality Traits
- Your Aspirations

- Your Dreams
- Your Values
- Your Beliefs
- Your Gifts
- Your Thoughts

> ❦ *The only things that can truly define you are within you.* ❧

There are many other elements that make up one's identity. We will discuss these aforementioned elements since these are not dependent upon outside forces, but are reflective of you as a person regardless of your profession, possessions, accomplishments or relationships. Thus, these are some of the factors we will explore throughout this book.

Identity Crisis

When we don't know who we are, we essentially have what is called an *identity crisis*. An identity crisis can happen to anyone at any age. How do you know if someone is having an identity crisis?

Here are a few possible symptoms of an identity crisis:

- Not knowing what you want in life
- Not having a preference or an opinion
- Not knowing your strengths or talents
- Feeling inauthentic, pretending to be something you're not
- Fear and insecurity
- Feeling stuck
- Feeling lost
- Feeling hopeless/worthless
- Not knowing what you're here to do/No sense of purpose
- Feeling like you're not adding value
- Feeling like you're living out someone else's dream
- Not feeling connected to your work or your environment
- Sadness or depression
- Feeling trapped or like you're living in a cage
- Feeling like a zombie, like you're not living, you're just existing
- Feeling like you are not living out your own happiness or comfort
- Feeling jealous of others

The Severity of an Identity Crisis

An identity crisis is a serious matter. Many individuals are not sure of their identity and they have the potential to feel a sense of despair and hopelessness. When people feel disconnected from the world, and unsure of how they are uniquely designed to fit in the world, they can develop negative and potentially destructive behavior patterns.

Negative habits that can develop when people experience an identity crisis:

- Negative Thoughts
- Fear/Anxiety
- Restlessness
- Depression
- Overeating
- Overspending

- Addictions
- Apathy
- Rebellion
- Comparison
- Aggression
- Substance Abuse
- Promiscuity
- Jealousy
- Reclusion
- Fantasy

Types of Identity Crisis

There are different types of identity crisis that exist and could affect individuals at any age or phase of life. While there are many types of identity crisis, two types that could affect individuals at a certain age in life are the Quarter Life Crisis and the Mid Life Crisis.

The Quarter Life Crisis

The quarter life crisis could occur somewhere around the age of 25. It occurs after individuals have begun in the workforce and they realize they are not happy with the career they have chosen. They may have pursued a career for money or because others encouraged them to pursue it. For several years, they may have pursued dreams, goals and activities that were not in line with their own personal desires or strengths. Perhaps they followed someone else's dreams for their lives. After they have worked for a few years, they realize they are not only unhappy and unfulfilled, but they are not sure who they truly are or what they really want in life.

The Mid Life Crisis

The midlife crisis could occur somewhere around the age of 50. It occurs after individuals have spent several years working in a profession that may be unfulfilling, raising children or doing something that is contrary to what they preferred to do with their life. They may have continued on that path in order to pay the bills, to provide for a family, or to please others.

Once they realize they have spent a lifetime pleasing everyone else, they may begin to question who they are, outside of their responsibilities to others. As a result, they may begin to pursue their passions and make life changes that allow them to feel a sense of joy and fulfillment as a reward for their hard work.

There are many situations that can cause someone to feel lost and unsure about who they are. Here is a list of several other events that can potentially cause individuals to have an identity crisis:

- Marriage
- Divorce
- Empty Nest
- Going Away to College
- Career Change
- New Environment
- Sudden Job Loss
- Abuse
- Abandonment
- Death of Loved Ones
- Homelessness
- Failure/Loss
- Promotion/New Job
- Periods of Unemployment

When we know who we are, we can be secure in knowing our identity remains solid, while the circumstances around us may change. This is the process of living authentically.

Authenticity

Authenticity is about knowing your true self and being able to move freely and confidently in the world. When you know your authentic self, even though the circumstances around you may change, the essence and core of who you are does not change. You remain solid.

Authenticity and Power

Our self worth and our personal power do not come from what we do but rather who we are inside. That is where our real power lies. Once we know who we really are, we can then affect real change in this world from an enlightened and empowered place within ourselves. Nothing can shake us or break us down because we know who we are. If we make a mistake, we know that mistake is not who we are. If someone else criticizes us, we know that criticism or judgment is not who we are but rather a reflection of the other person's perception. We no longer react to the things that happen outside of ourselves because we are firm in our foundation within.

Authenticity and Purpose

When you know your identity, you don't have to try as hard to find purpose, it will find you. However, it is important to remove the masks and false identities in order for your purpose to find you. There is a specific assignment in this world that only you can fulfill. Everything that you are searching for is also searching for you. So, since your purpose is searching for you, it may not be able to find you if you don't know who you are. It is important to remove the layers of false identity we are currently holding onto. Once you begin on the journey to uncover your true authentic self, everything else will begin to flow to you.

> *Everything you are searching for is also searching for you.*

Embracing our uniqueness is the key to unlocking every good thing life has for us. There are wonderful things waiting for you in the world, but they cannot locate you until you discover who you truly are. Once you fully understand your identity and embrace it, then you can position yourself to attain everything life has for you. However, if you continue to hide or pretend to be something that you are not, you will continue to live beneath the potential already predestined for you alone.

When we try to pretend that we are just like everyone else, or pretend to be someone else, we are attempting to avoid the risk of rejection to ensure success. When we don't take the time to discover our true selves, we stifle our own amazing identity and personal power, and thus miss out on the treasures that await us.

In order to begin to achieve our true authenticity, we need to let go of:

- False identities
- Labels
- False responsibilities
- Guilt
- Manipulation
- Control
- The Past
- Blaming Others
- Fear
- Masks

- Negativity
- Limiting Beliefs
- Bad Habits
- Hiding
- People Pleasing
- Other People's Problems
- Unforgiveness
- Complaining
- Hurt/Pain
- Shame

Creating Identity

When we talk about ourselves to others, we create our identity. No one has more power to create your identity than you. We must be aware of the language and vocabulary we use when we talk about ourselves. Many times we say things like, "I am afraid," or "I am a mess". I AM statements are some of the most powerful statements we can make about ourselves, because they become a part of our identity.

PROSPER ON PURPOSE

We must remember that we are *not* our feelings, emotions or even our actions. It is possible for us to "feel" afraid, but not "be" afraid. It is even possible for us to treat someone in an unkind way, but to not "be" unkind. That is not who we really are, it is just a feeling or an action. Remember, your emotions, feelings, thoughts, actions and current state in life can be temporary and will pass. However, when we speak about ourselves, we want to use words that speak to who we are at the core of our being. These words will endure even though our circumstances may pass.

Labels

Labels are words and thoughts that others say or think about us that are not true. When we allow these to stay with us, and don't challenge them, they become a part of our identity and cause damage. We then believe we have to become what was said about us. We have the power to remove these labels from ourselves, thus freeing ourselves to develop into the true version of our authentic identity.

Judgmental people live life in chains. They are in bondage to their own thoughts, opinions and way of viewing others. Whenever you judge someone, not only do you attempt to put chains on someone, but you also become chained to that very same judgment and perspective.

You don't have to accept the chains of what others think of you. Some of us have let others put labels on us in the past. When you realize you have the power to walk away from other people's judgments, leaving them holding their own chains, then you will live life in freedom. You don't have much control over what people think of you. What they think of you represents their own view of life and the world. This does not have to be your reality. Don't allow yourself to be dragged down by other people's negative view of the world or their view of you. Knowing who you are will help you to walk in confidence and self assurance no matter what others say about you.

MELODY THOMPSON

Personal Brand Identity

While you may use several words to describe yourself, most likely others will associate you with one to two words, which is called your personal brand identity. Your personal brand identity consists of the words or phrases others use to describe you, making it simple to know why you are unique. We all have a personal brand that tells the world who we are. If we don't create and control our personal brand identity, others will create it for us and they will determine who they think we are. Your brand identity can identify how you want others to see you and how you would like to represent yourself in the world. This should naturally flow from our true authentic identity and not a mask of who we pretend to be.

False Burdens

False burdens are unnecessary expectations that other people place on us, which affect who we are. Burdens can be passed down generationally or we can take them on ourselves. We may be holding on to the pain of our family members, our parents or even our ancestors. When we frequently take on other peoples' problems, it becomes a burden in our lives. False burdens exist when we feel a need to help others excessively or make them happy when they are experiencing pain or sadness in their lives.

Due to our compassionate and loving heart, we become weighed down when others show a lack of motivation to fix their own problems. There is nothing wrong with helping those in need, as we all need a helping hand every once in a while. However, to consistently take on other peoples' burdens may create a false idea that you should take care of others who are capable of caring for themselves.

We cannot change people and it becomes a burden to constantly try to fix their issues. These burdens weigh us down, hold us back and keep us stuck in life. We may even feel these burdens become a part of our identity, and they begin to affect our actions and how we see ourselves. We were not designed to carry other people's weight. It is difficult enough for us to bear our own problems. So, we have to let go of false burdens which create false identities. Instead, we must discover who we truly are and what we are meant to do in life.

Activity: Create Identity Statements

You will create I AM identity statements that describe who you are. Make sure your I AM identity statements reflect who you truly are on the inside. Avoid mentioning material possessions, physical attributes, external situations, bad habits, past failures, labels, temporary settings, negative words or relational connections.

Your I AM statements will come from who you are inside – your best authentic self. Your statements should be positive, future focused, authentic, true and realistic. You may list descriptive words as well as titles. For example you could say – "I am a teacher", or "I am an advocate", to describe who you are and what you provide in the world.

Use the list of personality traits on the next few pages for ideas for descriptive words.

Self Discovery Questions

1. Who are you? How do you define yourself?
2. Identify 10 words that describe who you are.
3. Pick your top three.
4. What are some of your best personality traits?
5. What life experiences have positively or negatively influenced your identity?

6. Are there any false identities you or others have created for yourself? Are you willing to let go of them?

7. What material things have you used in the past to define your identity?

8. What do you need to eliminate in order to become your authentic self?

Assignment

Personality Tests

- Free Personality Test: https://www.16personalities.com/
- Free Personality Test: http://www.my-personality-test.com
- Free Personality Quizzes - https://www.visualdna.com/quizzes/

Personality Traits

Able	Caring	Direct	Glorious
Accepting	Cautious	Diplomatic	Good
Accomplished	Centered	Disciplined	Graceful
Accurate	Certain	Discrete	Gracious
Achieving	Charitable	Discriminating	Grateful
Adaptable	Charming	Driven	Great
Adorable	Cheerful	Dynamic	Grounded
Adventurous	Classy	Eager	Guiding
Affectionate	Clean	Educated	Handsome
Alert	Clear	Efficient	Happy
Alive	Clever	Elegant	Hard-working
Altruistic	Colorful	Empathetic	Harmonious
Amazing	Committed	Encouraging	Healing
Ambitious	Communicative	Energetic	Healthy
Analytical	Compassionate	Enlightened	Helpful
Appealing	Compatible	Enthusiastic	Hilarious
Appreciative	Competitive	Excellent	Honest
Artistic	Complete	Exciting	Hopeful
Aspiring	Confident	Experienced	Humble
Assertive	Conscientious	Fair	Humorous
Astonishing	Considerate	Faithful	Idealistic
Attentive	Consistent	Family-oriented	Imaginative
Attractive	Content	Fashionable	Incredible
Aware	Cooperative	Favored	Independent
Awesome	Courageous	Feeling	Industrious
Balanced	Courteous	Flexible	Influential

MELODY THOMPSON

Beautiful	Creative	Flourishing	Innovative
Blessed	Cuddly	Focused	Insightful
Blissful	Curious	Forgiving	Inspirational
Bountiful	Cute	Free	Inspired
Brave	Decisive	Fresh	Intelligent
Bright	Deep	Friendly	Intense
Calm	Delicate	Frugal	Interesting
Candid	Delightful	Fun	Intriguing
Capable	Dependable	Funny	Introverted
Captivating	Desirable	Generous	Intuitive
Carefree	Determined	Gentle	Inventive
Careful	Devoted	Giving	Invigorating
Involved	Peaceful	Self-confident	Talented
Jolly	Perceptive	Self-directed	Tenacious
Joyful	Persevering	Self-disciplined	Tender
Just	Persistent	Self-reliant	Terrific
Kind	Persuasive	Selfless	Thorough
Leading	Phenomenal	Sensitive	Thoughtful
Learned	Playful	Serene	Thought Leader
Logical	Poetic	Serious	Thrifty
Loving	Polite	Sexy	Thriving
Loyal	Popular	Sharp	Tolerant
Lucky	Positive	Silly	Tough
Luxurious	Powerful	Simple	Trusting
Magical	Practical	Sincere	Truthful
Magnificent	Precious	Skilled	Trustworthy
Manly	Precise	Smart	Unassuming
Masculine	Professional	Smooth	Understanding
Mature	Profound	Soft	Unpretentious
Meek	Progressive	Sophisticated	Unselfish
Modest	Proud	Special	Unwavering
Moral	Punctual	Spectacular	Uplifting

PROSPER ON PURPOSE

Motivated	Pure	Spiritual	Useful
Motivating	Purposeful	Splendid	Valuable
Natural	Questioning	Spontaneous	Verbal
Neat	Quiet	Stable	Vibrant
Nice	Ready	Steadfast	Victorious
Noticeable	Realistic	Simulating	Virtuous
Nurturing	Refreshing	Strategic	Vital
Obedient	Reliable	Strong	Vivacious
Objective	Resilient	Strong-willed	Warm
Open	Resourceful	Stunning	Wealthy
Open-minded	Respectful	Stylish	Whole
Optimistic	Responsible	Successful	Wholesome
Organized	Responsive	Supportive	Willing
Original	Rich	Supreme	Wise
Outgoing	Romantic	Surprising	Witty
Outstanding	Royal	Sympathetic	Wonderful
Passionate	Secure	Systematic	Worthy
Patient	Self-aware	Tactful	Youthful

All About Me

Use the following questions to learn more about yourself:

Favorite Color(s)
Favorite Food(s)
Favorite Dessert(s)
Favorite Places to Go
If I Could Be Any Animal I Would Be....
Superpowers I Would Want to Possess

5 Things that Make Me Feel Happy
5 Good Gift Ideas for Me
5 Activities I Like to Do for Fun
5 Ideas for the Perfect Date Night
5 Things Most People Don't Know About Me
5 Things Most People Misunderstand About Me

5 Words to Describe Myself
5 of My Best Features (physical or personality)
5 Strengths/Things I Do Well
5 Words I Want Others to Say About Me
What is Most Important to Me in Life

5 Things that Make Me Feel Sad
5 Things that Make Me Feel Angry/Frustrated in Life
5 Things I Hate Doing
5 Weaknesses/Things I Don't Do Well
Things That Are Not Important to Me in Life

PROSPER ON PURPOSE

Where I Want to Be in 1 Years
Where I Want to Be in 5 Years
Where I Want to Be in 10 Years

Greatest Desire/What I Want Most In Life
My Deepest Fear(s)

I feel most comfortable when…
I feel most uncomfortable when…
I feel most confident when…
I feel most insecure when….

What I need the most help with in life
What I feel I can help others with most in life

TAGS™ - Talents, Abilities, Gifts, Skills

Identifying Your TAGS™ – Talents, Abilities, Gifts, Skills

We have all been given some type of talent or ability in our lives. We may have heard different words to describe talents and abilities however many people may not be able to distinguish the difference between them. We will discuss your TAGS™ – Talents, Abilities, Gifts and Skills and the differences between them.

Talent

A talent is a natural inclination to do something extremely well, that others may have to work hard to achieve. This can be what you do for a living, such as your paid profession. However, while it may be a clue to your purpose, it may not be the full extent of your purpose. A talent is something you do well, which has the potential to run in the family. Many families are naturally talented in a particular area and it is often handed down through the family. There are athletic families, entrepreneurial families, musical families, etc. An example of a talent is the ability to sing well or teach well.

Ability

Ability is something you are able to do, however it is not necessarily a gift or talent. An example of ability is being able to drive, speak, clean, remove trash, etc. You may or may not be good at it and it may not require much skill or talent in order to be effective. You may not even be particularly passionate about it. You just simply have the knowledge and ability to do it.

Gifts

A gift is a divine enablement given to you that is connected to a higher calling and can also be considered to be a clue to your purpose. Gifts tend to be very high level abilities for which you have no explanation of how you are able to do it. Gifts are to be used for a purpose greater than yourself in order to help, heal and serve others. Gifts may or may not be associated with a family talent or trait. You may be the only one in a family with that particular gift, it may be passed down from generation, or it may skip a generation. Some gifts can be as natural as breathing and can occur with little to no effort. Other gifts may need practice and development.

> ❧ A man's gift makes room for him and ❧ brings him in the presence of great men.

Gifts can be automatic in nature, where you don't seem to control it, it can be the effect you have on people when you come around and use your talents. Other gifts can require some work to develop them. You can be born with these gifts, or they can come alive over time. If you had a talent of singing well and you decided to sing for people who have been abused and as a result people felt a sense of emotional healing take place – that is your gift in operation.

Skills

A skill is something you learn to do extremely well, in order to improve your talent. When you spend a significant amount of time working, studying and practicing, you become skilled at something such as your job, trade, or hobby. Being skilled makes your talents greater and puts you at a huge advantage over others.

The most successful people in life study to become skilled in their talents. If you had a talent of singing, then studying to become a better singer would be an example of becoming skilled in your talent. This makes you better and increases your opportunities for success, as well as improves your ability to help others with your gift.

Gifts

In the previous section, we discussed the difference between talents, abilities, gifts and skills. In this section, we will take a closer look at gifts. Gifts are intended to be used for the benefit of others. Until we use our gifts to benefit others, we will find ourselves in a state of feeling "stuck". When we use our gifts, they make room for us to be successful in the world. Your gifts prepare you for greatness. Gifts seem to operate on a level higher than talents and have a greater impact.

Some people believe the key to their success is hard work, the right education, good connections, their family name, their money or their experience. While all of these are helpful, there are many people in the world that have these things and may not be successful.

A gift is different from a talent because oftentimes your gift works without you knowing how it works. Your gift begins to work when you use your talent. Your gift works to help, heal and serve people. There are different categories of gifts, which we will explore further in the next section.

The reason some people may not understand how you will be successful following your dreams and using your gifts is because they don't have your vision. Also, they may not be able to do what *you* do or go where *you* will go. They were not created to do so. They could not be successful doing exactly what you do because your gift makes room for *you*. When you use your gifts, your gifts carve out a unique space for you in the world to be successful. When you begin to use your gifts, you will notice people will begin coming to you for it and seeking you out.

PROSPER ON PURPOSE

When you let your light shine, the people that need *your* light will flock to you. There is a natural flow of resources, energy and focus when you use your gifts. Your work becomes effortless and you seem to have a never ending well of energy and resources to do your work. This is the sweet spot.

Here are just a few examples of gifts:

Positivity	Hope	Joy	Comedy/Humor
Inspiration	Physical Healing	Emotional Healing	Patience
Empathy	Compassion	Creativity	Good Judgment
Prosperity	Communication	Motivation	Leadership
Service/Help	Wisdom	Love	Planning/Organizing
Kindness	Peace	Confidence	Gentleness
Self-Control	Restoration	Courage	Counsel
Intuition	Intelligence	Beauty	Justice
Encouragement	Generosity	Understanding	Hospitality
Empowerment	Boldness	Friendship	Loyalty
High Energy	Charisma	Ambition	Strength
Liberation	Enlightenment	Influence	Elevation
Unity	Genuineness	Vitality	Altruism
Protection	Mercy	Vision	Advocacy
Favor	Growth	Faith	Reconciliation
Transformation	Development	Adventure	Health
Humility	Activism	Integrity	Curiosity
Connection	Resilience	Authenticity	Excellence

Your wealth is within you. Abundance flows out of you first, then back to you. It is the principle of reciprocity. What you give, you receive back. Even if you don't receive it back right away or from the place where you gave it, it will undoubtedly return. If it takes longer than expected to receive the good you have given, that only means it is gaining interest and when it comes back it will be massive. When you release the wealth that is inside of you, then tangible material wealth can flow back to you. The key to activating this principle is you have to release your treasures (your gifts) *first*. This is why it is important not to withhold or sit on your gifts because it can potentially block your flow. It's time to release and flow.

Four Categories of Gifts

Many people believe a gift is something that is automatic and does not need to be developed. However, there are many different types of gifts and some need development. We will discuss four categories of gifts below.

Distinct Gifts

Distinct gifts are gifts that are obvious, automatic and in operation at birth. You and everyone around you may know it is a gift from a very young age. It feels as natural as breathing and may even operate without you having to do anything at all. This type of gift tends to be effortless and can even feel out of control at times. You may not fully understand how to control it or harness it to use it for good, and it may cause you to be misunderstood early in life because of this reason. This type of gift makes you stand out and makes you different from others.

Examples of Distinct Gifts:

- Being very talkative in school = gift of communication
- Telling jokes in class = gifts of comedy and humor
- Being overly sensitive as a child = gifts of compassion and empathy

PROSPER ON PURPOSE

Developed Gifts

These types of gifts need to be developed, honed and trained in order to operate at their full potential. If you don't develop this type of gift, you may find that you remain average in this area. Although you have to develop these gifts and work on them in order to be your best, you don't have to try as hard as others in this area. It seems your work and efforts in this area are multiplied and you find twice as much success in this area as others around you who are not as gifted.

Examples of Developed Gifts:

- Leadership
- Patience
- Courage
- Intuition
- Confidence
- Wisdom

Discovered Gifts

These types of gifts are usually discovered over time through different experiences. You may not know you have this particular gift until you have a specific experience where it seems to appear out of nowhere. You will experience significant growth and favor in this area, even when others have been doing it for years.

Examples of Discovered Gifts:

- You are forced to give several presentations at work and discover you have a gift for public speaking.
- You decide to start a hobby of painting and discover you are a gifted artist.
- You are laid off from your job, and you are forced to start your own business. You discover you have a gift for business management and entrepreneurship.

Dormant Gifts

With these types of gifts, you don't know you have them until you're forced to use them. These types of gifts lie dormant and are reserved for certain circumstances. These gifts may not always be in operation, as they are not always needed. They come alive for specific assignments and situations.

Examples of Dormant Gifts:

- The ability to hear your baby cry from a long distance and know your child is hungry.
- The ability to learn and understand educational material very quickly and be able to teach it to others.

Now that we have explored gifts, let discuss another part of your identity, your intelligence.

Intelligence

Most of us at some point have taken an IQ (Intelligence Quotient) or an aptitude test as children. The result of a test score such as this is to give you an identity or ranking compared to your peers and determine how smart you are. It can be discouraging to children to evaluate their IQs. Regular school tests can have the same effect.

Intelligence is seen as a scale that simply goes upwards from average to smart or super-smart, or downwards toward below average. Most of us develop an identity based on this perceived level of intelligence, and we learn that this is something we can't change. It becomes a label we carry around with us.

Whatever we've been taught in our early education, whether it's "I'm gifted and the teacher likes me" or "I'm stupid and I'll never be a smart kid," can turn into negative self-talk. This is something that is very difficult to unlearn. Modern research shows that intelligence is much more diverse and multifaceted than this over-simplified system suggests.

Everything in this world is intelligent. Ants, bees, birds, horses, lions, flowers, trees and every other creation have a level of intelligence. Certain animals instinctively know how to hunt or gather. Bees know how to pollinate and make honey, while birds know how to create nests and lay eggs. Even plants, that appear to have no brain, know when to shed their leaves every fall, when to grow their leaves back in the spring and they even know what seasons to produce fruit. The sun rises every morning and she is never late! Every created thing is intelligent by design and you are no exception to that fact. You are incredibly intelligent and masterfully made.

There are different types of intelligence. You may have high levels of intelligence in one area or several areas, while you may seem to struggle in other areas. Your goal should be to discover the areas in which you are highly intelligent and seek to focus much of your time and effort on becoming proficient in those areas.

Types of Intelligence

According to Dr. Howard Gardner, a Harvard professor and developmental psychologist, in his book *Frames of Mind: The Theory of Multiple Intelligences,* he states there are nine types of intelligence.

The nine types of intelligences Dr. Gardner describes in his book are Verbal Linguistic Intelligence, Logical Mathematical Intelligence, Visual Spatial Intelligence, Musical Rhythmic Intelligence, Interpersonal Intelligence, Intrapersonal Intelligence, Existential Intelligence, Naturalistic Intelligence and Bodily Kinesthetic Intelligence. We may have one or more of these intelligences, which can help us define our identity and understand what we do best. We will explore each of these further to understand what types of intelligence we possess.

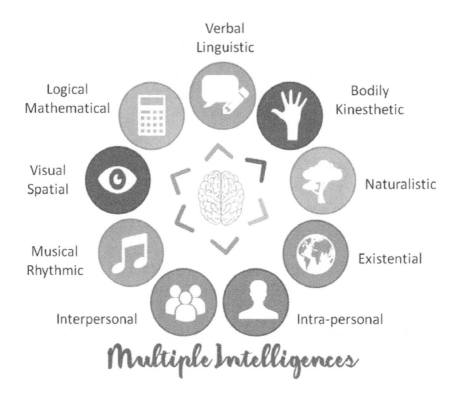

Verbal Linguistic Intelligence

Verbal Linguistic Intelligence is the ability to use words masterfully in order to create mental pictures and express complex information. Verbal Linguistic Intelligence allows us to understand the order and significance of words and to reflect on our use of language. Verbal Linguistic Intelligence is the most widely shared natural ability. This ability is seen in poets, writers, journalists and public speakers. Individuals with this kind of intelligence enjoy writing, reading, telling stories, speaking, talking or doing crossword puzzles. They prefer to use words in their learning and working style, by using speech, reading and writing.

PROSPER ON PURPOSE

Logical Mathematical Intelligence

Logical Mathematical Intelligence is the ability to perform complex mathematical operations such as analyzing, measuring and developing intricate calculations and hypotheses. This ability allows individuals to make logical connections and utilize abstract symbols, sequential reasoning as well as inductive and deductive thought patterns. Logical-Mathematical Intelligence is typically found in mathematicians, scientists, engineers, financial advisors, accountants, bankers, analysts, medical professionals and detectives. Individuals who possess this ability typically find themselves interested in patterns, data, numbers, logic, strategy, experiments and sequences. They typically prefer to utilize logic, reasoning, data, systems and process in their learning and working styles.

Visual Spatial Intelligence

Spatial intelligence is the ability to think creatively and conceptually in three dimensions. Core capacities include mental imagery, spatial reasoning, image manipulation, graphic and artistic skills and an active imagination. Artists, designers, sculptors, painters, sailors, pilots and architects all exhibit spatial intelligence. Young adults with this kind of intelligence may be fascinated with mazes or jigsaw puzzles or spend free time drawing or daydreaming. They prefer using pictures, drawings, images, and spatial understanding to learn and to work.

Musical Rhythmic Intelligence

Musical Rhythmic Intelligence is the ability to interpret and understand sounds, rhythms, resonance, pitch and tone. It is considered an auditory learning ability. This type of intelligence allows individuals to identify, develop, produce and reflect on sounds and music. Individuals with this ability typically include musicians, producers, composers, vocalists, conductors and those with an appreciation for the arts and music.

MELODY THOMPSON

There is a connection between mathematical and musical intelligences, as they often share common thinking processes. You may see individuals with this ability often moved by music and they seem to learn and work best with sound, music or even light noise in the background. You may even find them tapping rhythmic beats on the desk, humming or reciting rhyming verses. These individuals have a keen awareness of sounds and are able to identify what type of instrument was used or what sound was made, and even put sounds together to create beautiful music. Individuals with this ability prefer to use sound and music to learn and work.

Interpersonal Intelligence

Interpersonal Intelligence is the ability to effectively relate to others in a way that is compassionate and courteous. This ability utilizes verbal and nonverbal communication, compassion and empathy. These individuals have the ability to be sensitive to different personality styles and the ability to work with different perspectives. Individuals with this ability are typically considered leaders in their sphere of influence and possess the ability to understand the emotions and perspectives of others. This can also be described as Emotional Intelligence. Individuals with this ability can include leaders, coaches, counselors, teachers, social workers, politicians and even entertainers. These individuals typically prefer to learn and work in groups, or even in one on one settings.

Intrapersonal Intelligence

Intrapersonal Intelligence is the ability to deeply understand oneself, including one's emotions, thoughts and motives in order to plan and direct one's life effectively. Individuals with this ability have a deep appreciation and understanding of themselves as well as the human condition. This ability is often found in life coaches, counselors, therapists, psychologists, spiritual advisors and philosophers. Individuals with this ability tend to be deeply reflective, empathetic and self-motivated. These individuals typically prefer to work alone and choose self-study as their preferred method of learning.

Existential Intelligence

Existential Intelligence is the ability to ponder and understand the deep questions of human existence, the meaning of life, the creation of humanity and the afterlife. Individuals with this ability tend to feel drawn to careers as philosophers, ministers, teachers and spiritual advisors. Individuals with Existential Intelligence enjoy learning and working with abstract, deep spiritual matters and enjoy teaching others what they have learned. These individuals typically prefer to learn and work with spiritual and philosophical information and tend to spend time in deep meditation, reflection, study, research, prayer and solitude. Much of their learning and work is done in solitude, while their teaching is presented to groups of people, whether through writing or verbal presentation.

Naturalistic Intelligence

Naturalistic Intelligence is the ability to work well with living organisms such as plants and animals and to understand and interpret the natural world such as clouds, rock formations, oceans, land and other natural landscapes. Individuals who possess this ability may have careers such as botanists, oceanographers, geologists, archeologists, meteorologists, gardeners, farmers, park rangers, veterinarians, animal trainers, and natural scientists. Individuals with this ability prefer to learn and work in nature or with plants and animals.

Bodily Kinesthetic Intelligence

Bodily Kinesthetic Intelligence is the ability to interpret and understand the world through bodily movements. Individuals with this ability possess great skill in controlling the body and handling objects with great skill. Those with this intelligence tend to need to use their hands and move frequently. Dancers, athletes, builders, artisans, massage therapists, craftspeople and surgeons are some examples of professionals who possess keen Bodily Kinesthetic Intelligence. Individuals with this ability prefer to use their body and sense of touch to learn and work.

Additional Intelligences

There were a few additional intelligences considered by Dr. Gardner, after his book on Multiple Intelligences was published.

Teaching Pedagogical Intelligence

Teaching Pedagogical Intelligence is the ability to study, master, plan and teach educational content in a way that is relevant and engaging to the learner. This ability is typically found in those who have a teaching element to their work. These individuals seem to possess a natural ability to quickly absorb information and then produce learning materials that resonate with their audience and the result is actual effective learning by the students. There tends to be a connection with this intelligence as well as Verbal Linguistic Intelligence. Individuals with this ability tend to work as writers, teachers, professors, curriculum developers, philosophers or ministers. Other professionals may also possess this ability in order to teach others detailed information regarding their specific field.

Moral Intelligence

Moral Intelligence is the ability to discern and defend what is right and just in society. These individuals have a high quotient for morality, integrity, justice and abiding by the law. This ability is often demonstrated by judges, lawyers, activists, police officers, soldiers and spiritual leaders.

Flavor Intelligence

Flavor Intelligence is the ability to effectively combine diverse foods and flavors to create dishes that are visually appealing and flavorful. Individuals who possess this ability tend to study seasonings, flavor combinations, vegetables, meats and various cooking techniques. Typical professions that possess this type of intelligence include cooks, chefs, bakers, recipe developers, seasoning creators and the like. These individuals prefer to work with food, seasonings and cooking equipment.

Strengths

Your strengths are a summary of your talents, abilities, gifts, skills and intelligence that allow you to be your best in life. In order to be able to list your strengths, it is important to know who you are and what you have to offer. However, your strengths are not just the things that you do well, but they are the things that give you life and energize you.

You may have gifts and talents that you believe you are good at, but you do not enjoy doing them. These would not be considered strengths because they do not allow you to be your best. If you look at a task with dread, even though you are good at it, we will not consider it to be a strength.

> *The simplest and best definition of a strength is*
> *"an activity that strengthens you."*
> *And the proper definition of a weakness is*
> *"an activity that weakens you"* — *even if you're good at it.*
>
> – Marcus Buckingham

When we are using our strengths to pursue our goals in life, it will require us to step out of our comfort zone. Your comfort zone is the place that feels calm and familiar. When we are in our comfort zone, we may choose activities, environments and people who are familiar to us and who make us feel at ease. The problem with remaining in our comfort zone is we may miss out on situations that could enhance our abilities or opportunities to advance in our lives.

You may have heard the saying, *"A comfort zone is a beautiful place, but nothing ever grows there"*. When we seek opportunities to step outside of our comfort zone, we then step into the *growth zone*. The growth zone is where you will stretch yourself and reach higher levels of your potential. You may have to study, learn, try new things, go new places and interact with people you may have never encountered before.

It may often feel like a scary and uncomfortable place, as there will be some growing pains. However, the more we stretch ourselves the more we grow. The more we grow, the more comfortable we become. Your success is attached to your level of growth. There are some things in life you won't be able to receive until you grow and mature enough to handle them.

While we seek to step outside of our comfort zone to grow, we can stay within our *strength* zone to thrive. You may be challenged to take on new tasks and responsibilities in your work or in life, which may require you to step outside of your comfort zone. However, if we learn to stay within our strength zone, we can ensure we set ourselves up for success. Your strength zone is where you know you are gifted and talented. While you may take on a new task, your strengths will allow you to succeed in almost any environment because you know you are strong in certain areas.

If you step outside your strength zone, you may find you are not able to succeed at the level you would normally perform. In order to be successful, learn to step outside of your comfort zone in order to grow, but stay in your strength zone in order to succeed.

PROSPER ON PURPOSE

Strengthen Your Strengths

We all have strengths and weakness in our lives. Many times we are taught to strengthen our weaknesses. However, with this concept, we are learning to focus on something that isn't working. We tend to feel like a failure when we are not successful in strengthening a weak area in our lives.

In order to focus on what is working and improve our strengths, we are going to learn a technique called Strengthening Our Strengths™ (SOS).

The SOS technique allows us to focus on what is working in our lives, versus what isn't working. When we focus on what is working in our lives, and what we do well, it motivates and inspires us. We feel like we are winning and we tend to find more success in our lives. If we take an inventory of our strengths and then examine what we can improve in those areas, we will then be so strong, it will make it much easier to work on and eliminate our weaknesses.

Why focus the majority of our time and energy on things that don't work? It is best to find a workaround or help for our weaknesses and then focus our time and energy on improving our strengths. This will cause us to be unstoppable in areas where we are already strong. We are utilizing the power of concentrated effort.

When we focus our power, energy, attention and efforts in areas that will make a difference, then we will have the greatest impact. Now, this does not mean we will completely ignore our weaknesses. We just want to use the majority of our time improving what already works.

After we have improved our strengths, we can then focus on how to find help or improve our weaknesses. Working on our weakness in addition to our strengths will allow us to fully maximize our talents and improve our personal development overall.

Weaknesses

While we don't have to dwell on our weaknesses, it is important to examine them in order to ensure we present our best selves to the world. The sad reality is there are individuals who experience failure in life, not because they aren't talented, but instead because they lack the other critical personal or professional development skills they need to succeed. Your success in business or in life can depend upon your own honest examination of your weakness and making a commitment to improve in those areas of that threaten to jeopardize your success in the future.

Many individuals rely primarily on talent alone, however this may not take them as far as they would like to go in life. People who are far less talented but work extremely hard can become more successful and go further in life simply based on work ethic and developed skills. There may also character development skills needed for success.

There are others who are very gifted and talented, however they haven't learned how to treat others or control their emotions. They are not able to address others in a respectful manner and thus alienate their colleagues and hurt their opportunities for advancement. There are those who are talented and even socially adept, however they are morally and ethically bankrupt. These types of individuals seem to be successful for a period of time. However at the pinnacle of their success, it all seems to come crashing down, with much public embarrassment and shame once their poor character traits or unethical deeds have been uncovered.

Before we can be elevated to a place of leadership or responsibility, it is important to work on our character flaws that could potentially threaten our long term success. Professional and personal development is vital to our success in business and in life. These are typically the soft skills most employers look for when hiring employees. Many managers prefer to hire people who possess the character, temperament, personality and

PROSPER ON PURPOSE

professionalism necessary for the position and provide those people with the technical skills training needed while on the job.

So, essentially character is often preferred over talent, experience and education. We must take the time to take inventory of not just our strengths, but also our weaknesses in order to improve ourselves overall, thus increasing our chances for success, happiness and longevity in our lives.

Here are some common areas for personal and professional development:

- Leadership
- Problem Solving
- Empathy
- Social Skills/Networking
- Professional Skill Set
- Work Ethic
- Listening
- Emotional Intelligence
- Self Control
- Resilience
- Strategic Thinking
- Collaboration
- Time Management
- Productivity
- People Management
- Communication Skills
- Honesty/Integrity
- Positive Outlook
- Assertiveness
- Personal Responsibility
- Diplomacy
- Reliability
- Execution
- Delegation
- Decision Making
- Conflict Management
- Tenacity
- Team Building
- Personal Branding
- Attention to Detail
- Business Acumen
- Financial Management
- Planning/Goal Setting
- Confidence

Self Discovery Questions: Strengths

Discovering Strengths from the Past, Present and Future

Past

As you reflect on your past, what accomplishments make you feel proud?

Name some activities you were good at as a child.

What did you want to be as a child?

What did you get in trouble for as a child?

What valuable skills do you feel were overlooked and misunderstood by others?

What were you teased about as a child?

When have you been at your best in the past? What was the environment or situation?

What careers have you had in the past? Which allowed you to be at your best?

What careers were not the best fit for you? What are the reasons why?

What are some of the most common compliments you have received? How could you turn this into an opportunity to benefit yourself and others?

What lessons have you learned from the misfortunes you've experienced in the past?

How are you better because of those experiences?

Present

What gives you energy and excitement in your life?

What do you do that brings joy, helps people or makes others feel better?

PROSPER ON PURPOSE

What do people seek you out for or ask you to do for them?

What do others love or admire about you?

What types of people allow you to be your best?

What types of people don't allow you to be your best?

What types of environments allow you to be your best?

What environments don't allow you to be your best?

What time of day are you the most effective?

What do you do that makes you feel strong and powerful?

What do you do that gives you joy?

What are your pet peeves?

What are you able to do easily and effortlessly without much awareness that you are doing it?

What are you "overflowing" with, and can't seem to shut off? (Creativity, Business Ideas, Jokes, Teachings, etc.)

What words would you use to describe yourself?

What would you say are your best character traits and qualities?

What words would others use to describe you?

Future

How would you like to describe yourself in the future?

What do you have to change about yourself to become the "you" of the future?

Is there anything in your future that you feel happy or excited about?

What would you like to be able to master in the future?

Assignment: Strengths Test

Take the Strengths Test

http://richardstep.com/richardstep-strengths-weaknesses-aptitude-test/free-aptitude-test-find-your-strengths-weaknesses-online-version/

Activity: Strengthen Your Strengths

Use the SWOT Analysis charts on the next few pages to answer the following questions. The goal is to maximize your strengths, mitigate your weakness, manifest opportunities and manage threats.

1. List your strengths
2. What are the weaknesses you have in those areas of strength?

   (For example, if your strength is in communicating and speaking, one of the weaknesses of your strength could be that you talk too much! The threat of talking too much is you say the wrong thing or you alienate people. The opportunity you have is to work on listening more and talking less.)

3. What could you do to improve in those areas of your strength?
4. What other resources can you find to help you in your areas of weakness?
5. What would be the result if you improved those areas?
6. How could you adjust your working style to eliminate your weaknesses?

Self Reflection Questions

Strengths Reflection Questions:

1. Which of your strengths do you feel come natural to you?
2. Is there a common thread/theme to your strengths?
3. Which situations allow you to use these strengths?
4. Which situations hinder you from using these strengths?
5. How could you change your life in a way that would allow you to use these strengths more?
6. How can you combine several strengths and use them together?

Self Reflection Questions

Weakness Reflection Questions:

1. What are some areas of weakness that you can work on?
2. How could your weakness potentially threaten your success?
3. What are some ways can you work on your weaknesses to mitigate or improve them?

MELODY THOMPSON

SWOT Analysis

Complete a SWOT analysis of yourself.

Strengths	Weaknesses

Opportunities	Threats

Strengthening Your Strengths

How can you improve your strengths?

Strengths	Weaknesses of Strength

Opportunities for Strength	Threats of Strength

CHAPTER 2 – PERSPECTIVE

A belief is defined as acceptance that something is true or that something exists. It can also be defined as an opinion or strong conviction. Our beliefs shape our perspective, the way we view ourselves and the world around us. Beliefs can be developed from our family, our friends, society and our own personal experiences. When we experience something and we believe it to be true, then it becomes a belief system. This belief system then governs the way we conduct our lives.

When our beliefs are reinforced by our experiences, they become deeply ingrained in our lives. These beliefs then develop into deep seated beliefs or what is otherwise called faith. When our beliefs become deeply embedded into our lives, they seem to function on "autopilot" and they automatically create our world and the circumstances around us. If our beliefs are not true, they result in us living in a fictitious

"You become what you believe."

–Oprah Winfrey

reality that is less than our best in life. Therefore, the process of questioning and testing our beliefs will begin to reveal the truth to us and allow us to live the life we were designed to live.

Limiting Beliefs

Limiting beliefs are thoughts that hold us back from achieving our full potential. Often times limiting beliefs come from words that have been spoken about us or experiences we've had. We all have beliefs that either encourage us or discourage us. Healthy beliefs empower us by giving us life and energy, while there are limiting beliefs that discourage us and drain us of hope and confidence. We can have beliefs about ourselves, others, money, careers and even why certain things happened to us in the past. These stories we tell ourselves create our world and shape our lives. The good news is no matter what you have learned or experienced, you have the power to change your beliefs!

Where Do Limiting Beliefs Come From?

The first step in uncovering your limiting beliefs is to identify where the beliefs originated that are holding you back from achieving your vision for your life. Limiting beliefs come from various life experiences. They can even come from early childhood education. Generally speaking, society doesn't raise children to become adults who think like entrepreneurs. In order to fit into society as adults, we are conditioned to think in more fixed terms, especially as they relate to intelligence, money, and authority.

One of the main sources of limiting beliefs are the negative words that individuals in our lives have spoken over us. These can also be called *labels*. When we allow those labels to stick to us, we tend to feel powerless and weak. We are able to empower ourselves when we learn to reject and remove the labels and limitations others have placed on us. No one has the power to define you, you define yourself. This is part of the self empowerment process.

Possible sources of limiting beliefs:

- Family & Friend's Beliefs
- Educational Beliefs
- Community Beliefs
- Societal Beliefs
- Past Traumatic Events
- Past Failures
- Fear of the Unknown
- False Perceptions

Again, the first step is to become aware of the beliefs or attitudes that limit you. In order to do this, we need to look at where these mindsets originate.

Money

A key area of life where limiting beliefs hurt individuals is money and finances. These ideas usually originate within the family through the things that parents say to their children or through life experiences.

Common limiting beliefs include things like:

"Money is the root of all evil"

"People with money cheated to get it"

"There is never enough money"

"You have to sacrifice if you want to buy (enter any item here)"

"We'll never be able to retire"

These limiting beliefs express feelings of guilt, hopelessness, or scarcity about money. Obviously, these are feelings that are not useful for an entrepreneur.

Work

Early educational experiences can also play a part in shaping limiting beliefs about what "work" is. The current education system in most countries focuses on learning whatever is needed to pass an exam. It doesn't train children to become adult entrepreneurs, freelance workers, or leaders. As society changes, there is a lag in the education system, which is still following the old model.

Let's look at some common limiting beliefs on the next few pages. See if any of these resonate with you.

PROSPER ON PURPOSE

Common Limiting Beliefs

1. I'm not _____ enough (fill in the blank - good, educated, experienced, worthy, smart, rich)
2. There are too many people already doing this. I can't be successful.
3. I'm not well known or rich, so people won't listen to me.
4. So many others can do this better than me.
5. Why would anyone pay me this much?
6. Everyone must like me, love me or approve of me in order for me to be happy and successful.
7. I have to be good at everything the first time or else it is not worth doing.
8. They are more _____ than I am. (fill in the blank: beautiful, successful, liked, appreciated, experienced, etc.)
9. This is who I am. I can't change.
10. I'm not an expert.
11. I don't have enough time.
12. People like me don't do things like that.
13. No one I know is doing that.
14. What will they think or say about me?
15. I owe him/her/them.
16. I'm not good at that.
17. I can't live my dreams. That is for irresponsible people. I am practical.
18. It didn't work before, so it won't work now.

19. I have to be perfect in order for people to accept me or to avoid criticism.
20. When things don't go my way, life is terrible and seems to be hopeless.
21. My emotions are determined by the way people treat me or by my current circumstances.
22. What happened in my past represents what will always happen to me.
23. I need to make others feel happy so they will love me and I won't be rejected.
24. Other people have to approve of my idea in order for me to feel it is a good idea.
25. I can't trust anyone, or else they might betray me.
26. If I'm happy even when others are suffering, it means I don't care.
27. If I let people really get to know me, they won't like me.
28. I have to stay in the relationship because I can't make it on my own.
29. I can't be happy until the person or situation changes.
30. If they really loved me, they would have _____.
31. They did that to me because _____.
32. People always do this to me, and only me. They don't do this to anyone else.
33. People who do bad things are terrible people and should not be forgiven.
34. I need to do/be/have more to be worthy.
35. It is selfish to put my needs before the needs of others.
36. I'm responsible for making other people happy, and they're responsible for making me happy.
37. If I speak my mind, people won't accept me.

PROSPER ON PURPOSE

38. Compared to others, I'm not doing enough. I should be further along in my life than I currently am.
39. I am a failure because I failed in the past.
40. Their life is easier than mine. I had to work hard for everything, while they had things given to them.
41. If I could simply be more (beautiful, successful, likable, etc.) I would be happier.
42. I am not where I want to be in life because of him/her/them.
43. If someone else is very successful, that limits my ability to be successful and makes me a failure.
44. It's too late for me to find happiness and success in life.
45. I'd better not allow myself to be too happy, or else I will be disappointed.
46. I shouldn't have to ask people for what I want, he/she/they should know what I want/need.
47. My haters are my motivators and I need to prove them wrong. I let negative energy motivate me.
48. If I do exactly what they did, I'll have the same exact success.
49. I should be worried or afraid of stressful situations.
50. Rich people are sleazy and money is evil.
51. I have to work extremely hard for everything I get.
52. I'm the best in the world and no one can do this better than me.

Activity: Identify Limiting Beliefs

1. Identify 5 Limiting Beliefs that are holding you back.
2. Do you believe they are true?
3. What is your response to these limiting beliefs?

The Cycle of Belief

When certain events happen in our lives, they trigger an emotion within us. Those emotions then develop into thoughts, mindsets and beliefs about ourselves and our environment. Those beliefs create our actions and we must live with the results of those actions.

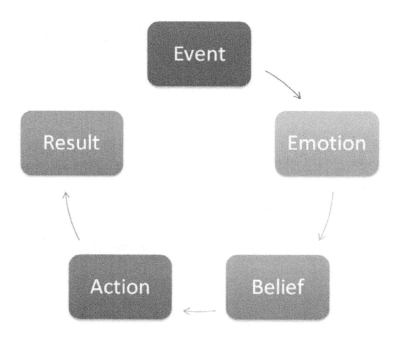

Identifying Limiting Beliefs

When we are identifying our limiting beliefs, look out for negative and absolute statements such as:

- Always
- Never
- Only
- Everything
- Nothing
- Everyone
- No One
- None
- All
- Can't
- Should
- Shouldn't
- Could
- Couldn't
- Every time
- Forever

When you, or someone else, frequently use these words they are indications of a limiting belief statement. These words create a sense that nothing is working and everything is hopeless, which may not be true. Limiting beliefs control our mindset and keep us stuck and subconsciously give us permission to give up and not try.

What Is Mindset?

Your mindset is a collection of beliefs. It includes beliefs about basic qualities like your intelligence, talents, and personality. The concept of mindset was first formulated and popularized by Stanford University psychologist Carol Dweck. Dweck's research focuses on the field of achievement and success. Her theory states that factors like intelligence and ability, while important, do not necessarily guarantee success. Rather, our mindset and our beliefs about our abilities play a key role in fueling, or dampening, our success.

All of us know someone who is incredibly intelligent or gifted but somehow never realized their potential. Think of a valedictorian who ends up working a dead-end job or a gifted athlete who gives up a sports scholarship in order to stay closer to home. These people seem stunted somehow and it's a great shock that they don't pursue their potential. It's easy to see that there's something holding them back that has nothing to do with ability or talent.

For example, you might have a certain view regarding your own intelligence. You may believe that you aren't "smart" because you didn't perform well in school, as it's widely believed that school performance equals intelligence. This may manifest itself in thoughts like, "I'm not smart because I didn't get good grades. Only smart people are successful. I am not smart and therefore my business will never be very successful." This negative thinking ignores the fact that intelligence means so much more than just school performance. Many people who did poorly in school went on to be great successes in their field.

Or you may have a negative mindset about your talents. You may be asked to speak at an event that could lead to great opportunities for your business, but you decline because of a self-limiting belief. You may think, "I'm not a good public speaker. When I presented my thesis in college, I choked. I couldn't remember words and I was too nervous to perform well. I'm just not a public speaker." However, public speaking is a skill that anyone can learn through practice.

Whether conscious or unconscious, these mindsets can directly impact your success. We've considered two examples that show how a negative mindset can hinder your success, but a positive mindset can help you activate your potential and reach heights of success you never imagined.

PROSPER ON PURPOSE

Growth Mindsets vs. Fixed Mindsets

Research about mindsets has identified two types – growth and fixed mindsets. The research has found that the more favorable mindset to cultivate is a growth mindset.

A fixed mindset means that you believe that your character, intelligence, and other abilities are static. This means that they are fixed parts of who you are and can never be changed.

A key characteristic of a fixed mindset is the need some people feel to constantly prove themselves. People with fixed mindsets often get consumed in proving themselves in class, in their jobs or in relationships.

This constant proving of yourself to others comes from the need to confirm your existing intelligence, talents, or abilities. This arises out of a concern over whether you will be perceived as smart or foolish, be accepted or rejected, succeed or fail. Individuals with a fixed mindset are overly concerned with the static labels they have come to identify with themselves, such as "intelligent," "gifted," "talented," and so on.

A growth mindset is one where an individual sees character, intelligence and abilities as always developing and evolving. Unlike the fixed mindset, a growth mindset doesn't compel you to constantly prove yourself because you know that you can change and grow with experience and practice. Your qualities aren't fixed. It doesn't matter if others see that you lack perfect qualities, because all of us are always growing, learning and evolving.

A key element of success in any field is the willingness and desire to learn new things and grow, and the acceptance of change. This is why a growth mindset is strongly associated with success.

A fixed mindset can be seen in a person who masters something quickly and then plateaus and fails to improve further. The person will either succeed with a task at first try or give up in disappointment. Their inner voice has already told them that they're either good or not good at the task at hand. A growth mindset can be seen in one who learns slowly and gradually, accepting new challenges and solving problems along the way.

These different mindsets can be recognized in early childhood. When given a challenging puzzle to solve, some children will try, fail, and become quickly disinterested and give up. Other children try, and even though they don't experience immediate success, they become engaged. They see it as a problem to solve and spend time with it. We often say kids like this love a good challenge.

These mindsets also reveal themselves to us later in life. Think back to someone you knew in high school that had everything going well for them. They were intelligent, talented, and personable and seemed to have everything in order. But in recent years, you reconnect with this person on social media or at a high school reunion. You're shocked to learn that their life took off early and then seems to have fizzled out or stagnated. While there are many reasons why things may not have worked out for them, it is possible this could be a person who has a fixed mindset and could not continue growing and evolving in the way that you expected.

On the other hand, if you reconnect with someone who has a growth mindset, they might have gone on to achieve more than you ever expected. The person may not have seemed like the type who was destined for great things, but over time, they might have started a business or achieved great success elsewhere due to the willingness to grow and stretch themselves.

PROSPER ON PURPOSE

Here is a summary of the key characteristics of the fixed vs. the growth mindset.

Fixed Mindset	Growth Mindset
Intelligence, character, and abilities are fixed	Intelligence, character, and ability can be developed
Succeeds early on, but may stagnate or not reach their full potential	Continuously reaching for higher levels of achievement
A hunger for approval. A desire to appear intelligent and successful. A desire to have a good reputation.	A passion to learn and evolve with confidence and self assurance
Effort in a new endeavor is pointless. It is better to stick with what you know	With effort, practice, and persistence comes mastery
Avoids challenges	Embraces challenges
Avoids situations where they might fail. Failure diminishes their sense of worth and the idea that they are smart or capable	Learns from failure. Failure is an opportunity to stretch your abilities
Gives up easily when faced with obstacles	Persists in the face of obstacles
Ignores constructive feedback	Learns from feedback
Sees the success of others as threatening	Learns from the success of others

So far we've discussed fixed and growth mindsets as though they were permanent personality characteristics, but this is not the case. Mindset is situational. You may use one or the other mindsets in certain situations, as well as at different times of your life.

For example, when you're facing a new situation where you're unsure of yourself, you're more likely to adopt a fixed mindset. You may adopt more of a growth mindset in activities where you're more confident or experienced.

In any case, defaulting to a fixed mindset, whether situationally or for a large portion of your life, has the potential to limit your success, happiness or potential in the long-term.

Something that also affects our mindset is the judgment of others who criticize us and project their mindsets onto us. These individuals are not aware of what they are doing many times because they are not aware of the errors in their own mindset. For now, we will call these individuals "critics".

Dealing with Critics

Dream Catchers vs. Dream Snatchers

We all have dreams for our lives. When we share our dreams and visions with others, some people may support us, however others may not. In fact, there are people who may put down our dreams and tell us why we can't achieve them. We must identify those people who support us and encourage us in our dreams. We will call the people who support us, *Dream Catchers*. These are people who are able to catch our vision, support us, encourage us and possibly even help us achieve it. We may have friends, family members, co-workers, managers or teachers who will support us in our goals. Many people may not have a support system within in their inner circle. However, there are people you can add to your support system such as mentors and counselors as well as life, career or business coaches.

While it is nice to have others to support us, we must learn to support and encourage ourselves. When we can empower ourselves, we no longer need to rely on the approval of others in order to accomplish our dreams. It does not matter much what others think about us. It only matters what we think about ourselves. What we say to ourselves creates our deep seated beliefs, which ultimately creates our lives.

Those who try to bring us down and discourage us from accomplishing our dreams, we will call them *Dream Snatchers*. Many times people don't realize they are being a Dream Snatcher. People provide advice out of their own personal experiences. If they are not able to do something, or if they don't like the idea, they think about it from their own perspective. Many times they don't intend to be negative, however it still discourages us.

While not everyone intends to hurt us, there may be a few people in this world who are mean-spirited and wish to hurt us with their words and actions. We must learn to protect our ideas and dreams from being criticized and judged by others. Perhaps this may mean being selective about who we share our dreams with in the future. We must learn to let go of the damaging words they have spoken to us or about us in order to move forward without the weight of those words. We then must build ourselves up with our own beliefs about ourselves and our potential.

The Three Types of Critics

There are essentially three types of critics: hostile, harmless and helpful. Each type of critic has a different agenda and each type, except one, has something good to offer. It's important to understand and differentiate between these three types of critics, so you can quickly identify those who you should listen to and those who you should ignore.

1. *Hostile* – Today, these types of critics are referred to as trolls. This type of criticism has no objective or supportive reason. Instead it is designed to demean, hurt and undermine. You can recognize this type of critic because they are on the attack and trying to tear you down. Most often, these are the people you should ignore.

2. *Harmless* – People who offer harmless criticism typically aren't interested in hurting your feelings as much as they are trying to shed light on the truth and facts surrounding an issue. They may be natural objectors who simply like being a sounding board to bring out the different aspects of a situation. Their comments aren't personal at all, they're objective. It's important to listen to this type of criticism and also pay attention to the facts of the situation, while not letting their feedback offend you.

3. *Helpful* – Yes, critics can actually be helpful. People who offer friendly criticism are often your supporters. These people care about you and want you to succeed. They often use constructive criticism to build you up, not tear you down. They want you to make it in the world and sometimes their ideas are good and sometimes not. They may even admire you. You're more likely to listen to this type of criticism since it comes from known supporters and those close to you, but remember to ensure that the advice given is fact based.

To evaluate criticism, consider the following:

- Is there any truth to it? – List out the facts of the situation so that you can determine what is really true and what isn't.
- Can I change this? – If some good points have been made, can you make a change?
- Does it matter? – Does this issue really matter? If it's something from a hostile source, does it really matter what they think?
- How can I make this positive? – Now, how can you take the facts of the criticism and turn it around into a positive?

In each case you should always listen to the criticism with open eyes and ears, without being defensive. Each criticism has its own good and bad points, and while you can ignore the person giving the hostile advice due to their rudeness, do listen to what they say so that you can determine if there is any level of truth. After all, regardless of the reason for the critic to give you advice, as long as there is truth you can still find a way profit from it.

Sometimes Dream Snatchers can also be the nagging voices in our own heads that tell us we can't succeed in life. This voice can also be known as your "Inner Critic".

The Inner Critic

Your mindset and beliefs can be totally subconscious. It's not always easy to identify them, but it's important to pay attention in order to draw them out. For many people, a negative mindset manifests itself as an "inner critic." This is an inner voice or private conversation that occurs in your mind, on repeat mode, behind your conscious thoughts.

The inner critic can be described as that negative voice within our minds that belittles us and tells us we are not capable of achieving our goals. The inner critic is like the enemy within ourselves, which steals our joy and holds us back from achieving greatness. It seeks to sabotage our efforts to move forward and succeed in life. In order to achieve sustainable success in our lives, we must defeat the enemy within ourselves and silence our inner critic.

Your inner critic may tell you that you're not good enough, you're bad at the task at hand, you're inadequate, or you lack the worth you see in other successful individuals. It acts as a judge, condemning you and calling you a failure at every turn.

Some people are aware of this inner critic while others aren't. Even if you're aware of this voice, you may be unsure of how to deal with it. Many people believe that the inner critic is themselves talking. They mistakenly identify with it and this is why it's so good at sabotaging your life and thwarting your chances for success.

Changing Your Mindset and Getting Unstuck

The first step to overcoming your inner critic and cultivating a growth mindset for success is to become aware of these negative thoughts and the impact they have on you. Once you've become aware of this inner voice, you've taken the first step toward releasing its grip on you.

The wonderful thing about mindset is that it can be changed. It can be developed or evolved. The negative mindset that's holding you back was shaped through experiences in the past and learned ways of thinking. Through even the smallest shifts in awareness or thinking habits, you can make profound differences and eventually take control of your mindset and steer it toward positivity and success.

When we listen to our limiting beliefs and fixed mindsets, they leave us feeling stuck and out of alignment in our lives. The ALIGN Method™ is a model I created to help you to align with your authentic self and the truth about your situation. This method will help you to identify and challenge limiting beliefs that are keeping you stuck.

ALIGN Method™ for Changing Mindsets

1. *Assess the Situation* – Ask yourself, where am I stuck? What am I thinking? How are my thoughts making me feel?

2. *List Your Beliefs* – What is the limiting belief? What do you believe about yourself or the situation?

3. *Identify the Source of Your Beliefs* – Where is this belief coming from?

4. *Gain Insight* – Gain insight on your belief by gathering facts, research, data. Is this belief true?

5. *Nurture New Beliefs* – Nurture new habits and new positive beliefs while also nurturing yourself.

PROSPER ON PURPOSE

Let's further review the steps in the ALIGN Method™ that will help you to conquer your inner critic, get unstuck and change your fixed mindset into a growth mindset:

ALIGN Method™ for Changing Mindsets

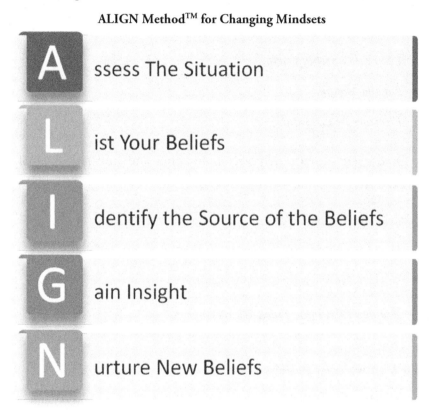

A ssess The Situation

L ist Your Beliefs

I dentify the Source of the Beliefs

G ain Insight

N urture New Beliefs

Step 1 – Assess the Situation

In order to silence our inner critic, we have to recognize its voice when it is speaking to us. It is also important to recognize the situations in which it shows up. To do this, you simply need to practice awareness and assessing the situation. Try to remember what event preceded those negative thoughts. It's a bit like trying to identify what is causing a stomach ache. You have to go back and try to remember what you ate just before.

When do you hear this voice? What does this voice say to you about yourself? Your potential? Your relationships? What negative results seem to come about as a result of listening to the inner critic's voice? Does it sound negative, condemning, judgmental?

For Example:

"I'm stupid."

"I can't do anything right."

"No one likes me."

"I'll never be successful."

Or does it sound overly accommodating and understanding of your flaws and trick you into staying complacent and remaining the same?

For example:

"You don't need to change at all, you're fine the way you are."

"Spending this money will make you feel happier."

"You don't have any issues. It's everyone else."

Step 2 – List Your Beliefs

In order to distinguish the inner critic's voice from our own, list out your beliefs. After you have written out your limiting beliefs, now write the beliefs down as "You" statements instead of "I" statements. This helps us to identify the inner critic as an internal enemy that has invaded our thoughts, and not our own voice.

If we can see the inner critic as an "inner hater" that tries to attack us and diminish our sense of worth from within, perhaps we can learn to reject its words and realize it is only lying to us. We can then silence its voice and seek the truth about who we truly are. Also, try to identify when these thoughts tend to arise.

List Your Beliefs

"I" statements	"You" Statements
I'm stupid.	*You're* stupid.
I can't do anything right.	*You* can't do anything right.
No one likes me.	No one likes *you*.
I'll never be successful.	*You'll* never be successful.

Step 3 – Identify the Source of Your Beliefs

If you're not sure you've identified your inner critic yet, try looking for triggers. For example, look for times when you find that you're doubting yourself, saying something like, "Can I really do this?" Or be aware of when you're focusing on failure rather than success. For example, perhaps you're worrying about what will happen if you fail at something. Paying attention to this feeling when it occurs will also help you identify the source of your beliefs.

Another good place to look for your inner critic's voice is any time you're trying something new or challenging. These are the most common situations where this negative voice arises.

Questions to Recognize The Inner Critic:

- Where did these thoughts originate?
- In what situations does the inner critic show up in your life?
- Is it triggered when you are around certain types of people?

- Who made you believe these things about yourself, your abilities, about others or about life?
- Is there an event in your life that caused you to believe this way?
- What triggers it? An emotion, an event, an action?
- At what types of events does it show up? On the job? In groups of people? When you're alone?
- What makes it louder?
- What silences it?
- Is this belief true?

Step 4 - Gain Insight

Once you know what your thoughts are and you have an idea of where they come from, it's time to gain insight on them and do some fact checking. Sometimes we have been told something when we were young, by people in authority, and we naturally believed it. When this happens, we tend not to seek out information to find out if it is true or not. Many times we spend years of our lives believing things that are not true, simply because we never gained insight on what was said. Or, we may have had experiences in our lives that taught us to believe something that is not always true in every case.

So, in this step we are seeking information, which could present truth to dispel the myths we've been taught in our past. These insights could come from any of the following places: books, courses, experiences, articles, examples, quotes, encouragement, coaching, counseling, advice, spiritual beliefs, mentors, friends, family, people of other cultures and others with a different perspective.

We can even gain insight on the belief by searching within ourselves, asking reflective questions and seeking the truth. After you have gained insight on this belief, then you can rate how true or intense that belief still is for you. You may then determine what you actually believe, based on your own current experiences instead of what you were taught or what you have experienced many years ago in the past. Once you have done this, you are ready to create and nurture new beliefs.

Gain Insights on Limiting Beliefs by Asking:

- What is the belief you have? Why do you believe this?
- Is this belief true? How do you know if this is true?
- What evidence do you have to support that belief?
- Are you willing to seek experiences and information to test your belief?
- Where can you gather evidence and seek the truth?
- Could the opposite be true?
- Have you ever tried anything to test the truth of what you believe?
- Has there been a time when this situation was different?
- How is your belief serving you?
- Do you think that your belief can be changed? Are you willing to change it?
- What is the truth about your belief?

Step 5 – Nurture New Beliefs

Once you can recognize the inner critic's voice, you can learn to control it and change your inner dialogue. The way that you interpret challenges, obstacles or criticism is up to you. This is the most challenging step for many people. It is difficult to reframe the inner critic's voice when you have old habits and patterns.

It is important to learn to change our inner dialogue and create new beliefs. When we reject the words of our inner critic, we refuse to allow its words or labels to stick to us. We are intentionally and purposefully choosing to come out of agreement with its lies and deceptions. We respond to the inner critic by writing down a more truthful, loving and realistic view of ourselves. When we respond, we respond in the first person, with "I" statements. With these statements, we are able to take a more truthful and nurturing approach to ourselves.

Nurture New Beliefs

Inner Critic Statements	New Beliefs
You're stupid.	I may not do well at certain tasks at first, but I am intelligent and capable of learning new things.
You can't do anything right.	I may not do everything perfectly, but I have the ability to learn from my mistakes and get better.
No one likes you.	I may not be the most popular, but I am likable and I attract the right types of people into my life.
You'll never be successful.	I am hard-working and I always do my best. I am sure to become successful at the right time.

Those in authority know best.	While I respect those in authority, I also listen to my intuition that lets me know what's best for my life.
Money is evil.	I can create abundant wealth for myself and family with honesty and integrity.
I can't try something without having all the answers first.	I can learn as I go.
I should always follow the all the rules all the time.	I can operate with integrity and follow my instincts along the way.
I have to always be nice to everyone.	I can be kind, assertive and authentic with others while honoring my own needs and desires.
What if I fail? I'll be a failure.	All successful people have failures. I can learn from every situation I encounter.

Moving Forward and Taking Action

Now that we have separated ourselves from the inner critic and responded with truthful statements about ourselves, it is time to make changes to move forward in a positive direction. We have control over our actions and do not have to act on the suggestions of the inner critic. Once we are able to silence our inner critic and see areas where we can improve, we empower ourselves to move forward and not remain stuck. With a new perspective, we are free to pursue our dreams and goals without the chains of criticism and judgment holding us back.

The more action we take, the weaker the inner critic becomes. Action kills fear. Our actions become a reflection of who we believe we are, who we want to be and what we believe we can achieve. We can also develop positive affirmations that represent who we truly are. These affirmations encourage our growth and development beyond the negativity of our inner criticisms. What challenges can you take on in order to foster and nurture a growth mindset? What challenges have you been avoiding?

"It's the repetition of affirmations that leads to belief.

And once that belief becomes a deep conviction, things begin to happen."

– Muhammad Ali

For example, you could connect with local entrepreneurs to create a positive peer group of people who have the mindset you want to develop. Or you could attend a conference or other networking event. Search online for opportunities to meet together with other like minded individuals.

Is there something you could delegate to someone else at work so that you can focus on more important things? What are some new skills you can learn and where can you learn them? Is there a particular risk or challenge your gut feeling is telling you to take? By actually getting out there in your personal life, your career or even as an entrepreneur, you'll provide yourself with challenges and learning opportunities that will have a transformative effect.

Choose a challenge and try it again, but this time, turn your fixed mindset around and silence your inner critic. Find a work-related or personal task that you've either been shying away from or that you feel you've failed at doing and try doing it with an open mind.

For example, perhaps you always put work first and your eating habits are not the best. How can you challenge yourself to create better eating habits? Maybe there is a skill you've wanted to learn such as cooking but the idea of trying again gives you a sense of anxiety. There might be an important client you've been meaning to contact but are avoiding it.

Start with one challenge, accomplish that goal and you can then tackle the next challenge once you have success with the first. Gaining small wins gives you the confidence and energy to accomplish bigger and more complex challenges in the future.

Self Reflection Questions

1. What is your limiting belief?
2. In what ways is this belief limiting you?
3. Is it true? How do you know?
4. What would your life look like if you held on to this belief?
5. What people, circumstances and unwelcomed situations have you allowed because of these beliefs?
6. How would you prefer to be, act, and feel?
7. What are the benefits of changing this belief? Imagine the best possible outcome.
8. What would your turnaround statement or affirmation sound like?
9. In what way does this affirmation reflect what you really want?
10. When will you start using the affirmation? For how long? How frequently?

11. Could you visualize the benefits you will enjoy with a new empowering belief? Visualize the new you and the benefits you will be enjoying with this new empowering belief.

12. How will you feel as the result of developing a new empowering belief?

Taking Accountability for Our Lives

"If you can't fly then run, if you can't run then walk, if you can't walk then crawl, but whatever you do, you have to keep moving forward."

- Dr. Martin Luther King Jr.

One of the ways we stay stuck is by viewing certain situations in our lives from the place of blaming others. Perhaps you have endured hardships and unfortunate situations at the hands of others. Although we may have been in situations where we did not seem to have any power to change things, we must realize we are not powerless in life. You are not hopeless or helpless; you possess a level of personal power within yourself to have an effect on your situation, even if it consists of simply changing your perspective on it.

While there may have been situations in our lives over which we had little to no control, many times we encounter situations where we do have control and the power to make changes. However, because we have been conditioned to feel powerless, we either allow others to make decisions for us or we blame others for the situations in our lives. Blaming allows us to stay stuck and remain powerless in life. When we blame others, it keeps us in a state of misery because we don't believe we have the ability to change anything, because it seems everything is always happening *to* us.

PROSPER ON PURPOSE

When we begin to take accountability for our own lives, we begin to experience the personal power we have to live the life we truly want. We must learn to stop holding others responsible for where we are in life. Even if others hurt us or held us back in some way in the past, we have the power to make a decision *now* to take accountability for where we are and where we want to go. It may be difficult to move forward, but any movement forward is progress in the right direction. The key is to not stay stuck on what happened in the past, but to move forward by recognizing what you can do today in order to change tomorrow.

Activity: Accountability Statements

In order to identify areas where we may not be taking accountability for our lives, we will create accountability statements.

Step 1: Choose a statement that describes a current problem you are having in your life.

Statement: *I am not where I want to be in life.*

Step 2: Rewrite that statement with the word "because". If your answer includes an outside force other than yourself, you are blaming someone or something else for the problem you have.

Statement: *I am not where I want to be in life because I didn't have the money I needed and my family members would not support me.*

Step 3: Now, rewrite that statement using the word "because", but now we will take accountability for our actions, instead of blaming others and outside circumstances.

Statement: *I am not where I want to be in life because I did not seek out the right people, help, resources and inner emotional healing I needed in order to move forward with my life.*

MELODY THOMPSON

We may have experienced tragedies and misfortunes in our lives. However, it is our choice to decide whether those things will hold us back or propel us forward.

Stories

In life, we tend to tell ourselves "stories" about why certain events happened to us. The stories we tell ourselves are always from our own limited perspective of what happened. Those stories may not even be true, but they inevitably shape the way we see ourselves and the world around us. Depending on the stories we tell ourselves, these beliefs can either help us to move forward or keep us stuck.

Many times, the things people do to us have nothing to do with us personally. However, it has everything to do with what is going on inside of the other person. Sometimes people do things to us because someone else did it to them and they haven't yet dealt with their pain or healed from it. Often times, people are busy, preoccupied with the stresses of their own lives and don't have the time or energy to give us what we need.

Other times, people do things to us not because they don't like us, but because they don't like something about themselves. They may see something in you that they wish they possessed within themselves. The bottom line is people can't give you what they don't have. If they don't love themselves, it will be hard for them to fully love you. If they are hurting, it will be difficult for them to give you what you need emotionally. I always say, "Someone with broken arms can't carry you". They need healing from their own brokenness first before they can adequately meet your needs.

When we are not able to let go of our expectations of others, we find ourselves disappointed and hurt. Our mind wrestles to find a reason why people hurt us. We as human beings are wired to think of ourselves first and we personalize situations that oftentimes have nothing to do with us. What others do to us, or don't do for us, is no reflection on us as a person or on our personal worth and value. You don't have to do anything to be worthy or valuable. You are worthy and valuable because you exist. People's actions toward us are a reflection of *the other person* and what is going on inside of *them*.

You never know what someone has gone through or is currently going through. It's not always about you. Sometimes we may expect people to give us things we may be able to give ourselves. This may include love, support, encouragement, confidence and the like. You have the ability to love and care for yourself, so you can relieve others of the burden of always having to fully meet your emotional needs when they are not able to do so.

We must learn to let go of our expectations of how we wanted others to treat us and remind ourselves to remain consistent in our identity and our character. When we maintain a positive self image of ourselves, we can remain consistent in the way we see ourselves and the way we treat others, regardless of how they treat us or what happens to us.

Story Examples

Story Example #1:

Story: *My parents resisted me and wouldn't let me do whatever I wanted to do because they didn't love me.*

Truth: Your parents wanted the best for you and wouldn't let you engage in self destructive habits.

Story Example #2:

Story: *My parents wouldn't support my dreams or my goals because they don't love me.*

Truth: Your parents wanted the best for you and were concerned about your future and your finances. They wanted you to be able to support yourself. They didn't know how it would turn out for you and didn't want you to be disappointed.

Story Example #3:

<u>Story</u>: *The woman walked right past me and didn't speak to me. She probably doesn't like me and thinks I'm beneath her. She's rude, stuck up and doesn't know how to treat people.*

<u>Truth</u>: The woman was in a hurry and didn't see you standing there.

Story Example #4:

<u>Story</u>: *She never calls me. She is a bad friend and doesn't care about me.*

<u>Truth</u>: Your friend is going through an intense time in her life and needs to focus all her time and energy on caring for herself, her family and her career.

Self Reflection Questions

1. What stories are you telling yourself about yourself? About others? About why things happened? About why people did something to you or didn't give you something you needed?
2. What do you think is the other person's perspective in that situation? How do they see it?
3. Are there any mistakes you might have made in the situation?
4. What is the truth about what happened?
5. What does this story allow you to avoid in your life?
6. What is the main emotion or belief that your story seems to support?
7. Who do you get to pretend to be by telling yourself, or others, this story?
8. Who would you become if you changed your story?

Significant Events

There are times in our lives where we have experienced a significant event. These events become etched in our memory and create beliefs about ourselves and our abilities. When these events are negative, we develop negative beliefs about ourselves. However, when we experience success, these events serve to build our confidence. Limiting beliefs are reinforced when we remember the negative experiences and forget the positive experiences that disprove the false beliefs.

One of the keys to overcoming limiting beliefs is to challenge our negative experiences and the beliefs those experiences taught us about ourselves. We can do this by remembering at least two to three experiences that were similar to the negative experience, yet they were positive. By recalling positive experiences, we begin to build our confidence and positivity regarding ourselves and our skills.

On the next few pages, we will take a look at some examples of significant events that may have created negative or positive belief systems. You will then list some of your own significant moments and events that have helped to shape your mindset.

The objective of this exercise is to focus on the positive events that dispel any limiting beliefs associated with negative events that occurred in the past.

MELODY THOMPSON

Here are some examples of significant events that may shape one's beliefs.

Significant Events			
Negative Event	Limiting Belief	Positive Event	Positive Belief
In 6th grade, I spoke in front of the class and froze up. The class laughed and I failed that assignment.	I'm no good at speaking.	I gave 3 speeches in high school that received applause from the class.	I am capable of speaking well with practice.
A friend betrayed me 15 years ago.	Friends can't be trusted.	I've made other friends who have been loyal to me.	People are human and make mistakes, but there are also good people in the world.
I started a business and it failed.	I'm a failure.	I helped other people's businesses generate millions of dollars.	I learned from my mistakes and now I'm better equipped for success.

PROSPER ON PURPOSE

Now it's your turn to fill in your significant events and beliefs.

Significant Events			
Negative Event	Limiting Belief	Positive Event	Positive Belief

MELODY THOMPSON

Negative Internal Promises™ (NIPs™)

Negative Internal Promises™ (NIPs™) are those silent agreements we make within ourselves to "never" do something in our lives. NIPs™ can be mistakes we've seen others make or they can be negative events we've experienced that we'd rather avoid next time. When we make these negative internal promises, we tend to shut down a part of our hearts in order to avoid these situations again. These negative promises ultimately close off our flow of abundance and begin to "nip" away at us. We then find it difficult to attain what we actually *do* want and we find ourselves inadvertently doing the very thing we said we would "never" do.

> "We waste a lot of energy trying not to be something.
> In order to not be something, I have to keep it in front of me
> so I can avoid it. The crazy thing is that
> I reproduce what I imagine.
> If I see what I don't want to be, just envisioning it
> causes me to reproduce it."
>
> – Kris Vallotton

These negative internal promises cause us to create negative feelings around things we want to change about ourselves or our lives. Instead of changing, we find ourselves drawn to doing the very thing we don't want. This is because our energy, thoughts and attention are powerfully and subconsciously focused on the negative things we don't want. Also, when we judge others negatively, life seems to have a way of letting us experience similar situations in order to teach us not to judge.

In order to see positive change in our lives, we can learn to focus on what we actually want to achieve and create positive affirmations or goals around it. It is also beneficial to learn how to empathize with others and learn from their mistakes rather than judging them for their shortcomings. This will allow us to focus on the positives and our true desires, in order to live a more free and fulfilling life.

Examples of Negative Internal Promises™ (NIPs™) and Goals

Negative Internal Promise™	Positive Goal
I'll never be broke another day in my life.	I will work towards having what I want and need in life.
I'll never depend on someone again in my life.	I will be self-sufficient in my life.
I'll never be like _____. I would never do what they did.	We are all human and capable of mistakes. I can learn from the mistakes of others and make wise decisions.
I'll never allow someone else to break my heart again.	I will take my time falling in love and using both my head and my heart.
I'll never trust anyone again.	I will be more discerning about my relationships.
I'll never let anyone hurt me again.	I will make sure I pay attention to the types of people I allow into my life.
Rich people are greedy and stuck up. I hate rich people and I never want to be arrogant and stuck up like them.	I want to be financially secure, generous, ethical and kind to others.

MELODY THOMPSON

Now it's your turn to fill in your NIPs™ and Positive Goals.

Negative Internal Promises™ (NIPs™) and Positive Goals	
Negative Internal Promise™	**Positive Goal**

CHAPTER 3 – PASSION

When people are passionate, they are able to do more and work harder with less stress. Even though they may put in more time to accomplish a task, it does not feel like work. For passionate people, work becomes more enjoyable and they are filled with energy, enthusiasm and satisfaction in their lives. Passionate people are inspired to continue learning and growing in their chosen field of work. As a result, they are happier, healthier, more fulfilled and more successful.

Passion filled people are individuals who have learned to be comfortable within themselves and thus have the knowledge of what is interesting to them and what ignites their passionate side. If you are looking to have a happy and fulfilled life, then it would be worth exploring the various ways you can pursue your passions and interests. Our passions invigorate us, excite us and bring us joy. When we follow our passions, we may find it is a good place to start on the journey to finding our purpose.

What is Passion?

Passion can be described as a strong feeling, desire or intense emotion about a person, thing or idea. Passion is motivated by what we like and what we enjoy doing. Our passions can be self-focused or self-satisfying. Our passions and interests may or may not be connected to helping others. Passion is rooted in the expression of deep emotions, which can serve to motivate us in our actions. However, with time, our passions can be subject to change depending upon the circumstances. While passion can be a step in the process of discovering our purpose, on its own, it cannot be considered our purpose.

Passion can point you to your purpose, but it may not fully consist of your purpose. Our passions describe what we like to do and what we enjoy. However, our purpose can entail much more than what we enjoy doing as a hobby, a pastime or even a career. Also, when our emotions and interests change, our energy to finish a certain endeavor can also fade. We must consider purpose to be a more permanent and lasting experience that overrides our emotions. Purpose consists of a dedicated commitment to a cause, no matter the circumstances or outcomes. Nonetheless, we will explore the areas of our passions and interests in order to gain a deeper perspective of ourselves and what we are motivated to do and create.

When you have passion, you have a vitality that allows you to achieve your dreams. Passion helps you get out of bed in the morning and seize the day! There are many benefits to being a more passionate person. With an invigorating passion for life, you can enjoy sustainable energy that motivates and inspires you. You'll also enjoy more leisure time, quality relationships, and people will be drawn to you. You'll also enjoy an enthusiasm for life that can last a lifetime. It all starts with passion.

Passion in Your Work

The most popular advice for career success is to find something you love, and then find a way to make money doing it. If you can find a way to support yourself working in a field you enjoy, most likely you'll get up every morning looking forward to doing something that hardly feels like work.

PROSPER ON PURPOSE

There may be times when you're stuck in a position that's less than ideal. If you explore the values and dreams within yourself and match them to particular aspects of your job, your daily grind can quickly turn into a daily pleasure. By finding deep meaning in what you do, your enthusiasm for work can naturally increase.

Passion in Your Social Life

When you find your passion, you can seek out others who share that passion. You can open yourself up to a whole new circle of people and experiences. When a group of people who share the same passion get together and talk about it interesting conversations can take place. Whether it's a vigorous debate or a networking event, it's always good fuel for your soul.

Discovering the passion inside of you makes you a more interesting person. Even when you're spending time with people who have totally different interests, you can exchange ideas on a whole new level and enjoy each other's company more when you have more to share.

Your friends, family, and colleagues may feed off your interest and enthusiasm. Your passion may become contagious, and you may win them over to your interests. With more in common, you'll experience a deeper relationship and more meaningful fellowship when you share your passion with others.

Passion in Your Hobbies

If you are feeling bored in your life, the best solution is to discover what excites you. Your passion is the fuel that ignites the joy you were created to experience. Infusing your passion into your weekly schedule, even in small amounts, can have a dramatic affect on the happiness you feel throughout the rest of the week. Find activities or hobbies that you can enjoy on your own or with others. This will help to invigorate you and experience joy.

Passion in Your Love Life

Knowing what your passion is can help you discover your potential romantic partners. If you find someone who shares your passion, or is at least supportive of it, you can develop a relationship where you can share your passion with someone who feels passionate about you.

Identifying Your Passions

Almost everyone is able to identify a hobby or an activity that keeps them happy, focused and feeling useful. This is a good place to start when it comes to finding our passions and interests. Sometimes, we have not identified our passions and interests, due to lack of exposure to various experiences. We are able to develop our passions and interests with increased exposure to different events. Understanding this may require us to take steps outside of our comfort zone, which is essential in the passion discovery process.

Being open to new experiences will help us to explore other possibilities that may surprisingly ignite the interests and passions hidden within us. There are many things to be learned when making the effort to engage in new experiences. If the results are positive and enjoyable, then we are able to explore these further and expand our level of expertise in these areas.

The challenge then becomes, how do you align your entire life so that you spend the majority of time engaged in the kind of work that makes you come alive? How do you find something that you are already good at, already enjoy and want to master? All it takes is the willingness to explore and try something new. If you are in a job you hate and have passion for something totally different, you don't necessarily have to quit your job. Instead, you can take on a small passion project, to which you can devote your spare time. Once you start along the path of exploration, you can create the momentum you need to change the direction of your life into a new, more exciting path.

PROSPER ON PURPOSE

For some people, it is easy to identify the things that make them happy and excited, while for others it may take a little time, effort and exploration. There is also the possibility that once identified, the activity that brings us joy and fulfillment may not be as profitable or needed by the general public. Once we have identified a passion, it is important to understand it may not necessarily be our profession or our purpose.

We may have passions that are personally fulfilling and satisfy a desire within ourselves, but they may not provide financial reward or serve as a way to help others. These types of passions are still worth pursuing and exploring for our own mental and emotional well being. We can then continue to explore other activities that are considered beneficial to both ourselves and others around us.

Self Reflection Questions

We will work through a series of questions to discover our passions.

Hobbies
- What activities do you enjoy doing?
- What could you talk about for hours?
- What types of books, articles or magazines do you like to read?
- What topics are you naturally drawn to in newspapers, magazines, on the internet or on TV?
- What are/were your favorite courses in school?
- What types of jobs or careers seem interesting to you?
- If you didn't have to worry about money, what would you choose to do for a living?
- What types of interesting activities do you spend large amounts of time doing?
- What types of charities or causes are you interested in donating to or helping?
- What type of information is interesting and fascinating to you?

- Who are your heroes and role models? What do they do?
- What activities are you doing that cause you to lose track of time?
- If you had no barriers or restrictions, what would you do?
- If you won the lottery, what would you do first?

Childhood

- When you were a child, what did you dream of doing when you grew up?
- What types of activities did you enjoy doing for fun as a child?
- What activities did you participate in at school?
- What types of games did you make up when you were a kid?
- What things did people ask you to do often as a child, that you were good at doing?
- What types of contests did you enter or win as a child?
- What types of awards did you receive as a child?
- What did people praise you for as a child?
- What made you stand out as a child?

Family

- What are some hobbies your family members have done?
- Is there a common career or profession that most people share in your family?
- Do people in your family share a common gift or talent?

Work

- What jobs have you held in your life?
- Which jobs did you enjoy the most? What parts of these jobs did you enjoy the most?
- What do you do easily and effortlessly that others find difficult to do?
- What do you do that seems like fun to you but seems like work to others?

- What types of environments do you enjoy working in the most? The least?
- What do people say are your strengths at work or on your performance reviews? Weaknesses?
- With what types of people do you work best?

Visions

- When you envision your future, what do you envision about yourself?
- When you see yourself in your dreams, do your dreams have a common theme?
- What good things have others spoken about your future?
- When you imagine your best self in the future, what do you see?
- How would you describe the life of your dreams?

Life

- When was the last time you felt alive and invigorated? Where were you? What were you doing? Who were you around?
- What thrills and excites you?
- What gives you a deep sense of satisfaction and fulfillment?
- What problems in the world upset you?
- What types of activities spark your creativity?
- What makes your heart sing?
- In what environments are you celebrated and not just tolerated?

Helping Others

- What are some common compliments you often receive?
- What do people often ask you to do for them?
- What ways do you often help people?
- What would others say you do well?
- How do you want to help people in the future?
- Why do you want to help others?

Connecting Your Strengths with Your Passions
- What would you consider to be your top 3 strengths?
- What would you consider to be your top 3 passions and interests?
- Where do you believe your strengths and passions are most aligned?
- What are the common themes you notice in the strengths and passions you have?
- What activities or careers allow your strengths and passions to come together?

Values

Values can be described as a set of beliefs and principles that govern the way we live our lives. Our values describe what is important to us and what influences our decisions in life. Values are important because they help us make decisions based on our principles and belief systems. While our values are defined by each of us as individuals, they can also be adopted from those around us.

Two types of values we will explore are Core Values and Inherited Values. Core Values are the values we feel are important in our own personal lives. These core values are the heart and soul of our lives and determine the types of choices we make. These values are used internally to act as a beacon and roadmap for our decisions. Inherited Values are the values we have learned from our parents, families, schools, friends, workplace or society. These values tend to relate to how we function in the world and relate to others around us. We may be taught these values or even adopt them based on our observations of others. We can review the values we have inherited from these different groups, in order to identify where they come from and see if they still represent who we are today.

Our values communicate what we believe and what we stand for. Values are essential to our personal success, because others make judgments and assumptions based on what we do, what we say and what we show them. We must ensure that our values match what we present to others in our actions.

If you're still confused when it comes to finding your passion, perhaps it will help to take an assessment of your values. In this section, you will have the opportunity to write down your values. When you see everything written down on paper it may provide you with some clarity. Everyone will have a different set of values; it's what makes a person unique. Once you've narrowed down your values, you can begin to determine how you can honor them each day. This can help you with gaining clarity on your passions, allowing you to find the commonality between your passions and your values.

Values Questions

List the values you gained from each of the following places:

- Family:
- Community:
- School:
- Work:
- Religious Group:
- Political Party:
- My Top 10 Personal Values:

1. Are there any values that no longer serve you? Can you let them go?
2. Do any of these values hinder you from living your best life?

MELODY THOMPSON

List of Values

Ability	Bliss	Connection	Dignity
Abundance	Boldness	Consciousness	Diligence
Acceptance	Bravery	Consistency	Diplomacy
Accomplishment	Brilliance	Contentment	Direction
Accountability	Brightness	Continuity	Directness
Achievement	Belief	Contribution	Discernment
Acknowledgement	Calmness	Control	Development
Adaptability	Camaraderie	Conviction	Discipline
Adequacy	Candor	Communication	Discovery
Adventure	Capability	Coolness	Discretion
Affection	Care	Cooperation	Diversity
Affluence	Carefulness	Community	Dreams
Alertness	Certainty	Competition	Drive
Aliveness	Challenge	Correctness	Duty
Ambition	Charity	Courage	Dreams
Amusement	Charm	Courtesy	Eagerness
Anticipation	Chastity	Craftiness	Economy
Appreciation	Cheerfulness	Creativity	Evolution
Approachability	Clarity	Credibility	Education
Artfulness	Class	Consensus	Effectiveness
Articulacy	Cleanliness	Curiosity	Efficiency

PROSPER ON PURPOSE

Assertiveness	Cleverness	Daring	Equality
Assurance	Closeness	Decisiveness	Elegance
Attentiveness	Collaboration	Decorum	Empathy
Attractiveness	Comfort	Deepness	Encouragement
Audacity	Commitment	Democracy	Endurance
Availability	Compassion	Delicacy	Energy
Awareness	Competence	Delight	Enjoyment
Awe	Concern	Dependability	Enlightenment
Balance	Completion	Depth	Entertainment
Beauty	Composure	Desire	Enthusiasm
Being	Concentration	Determination	Exactness
Being the Best	Confidence	Devotion	Excellence
Belonging	Conformity	Femininity	Excitement
Benevolence	Congruency	Masculinity	Exhilaration
Expectancy	Gentleness	Hard work	Neatness
Empowerment	Genuineness	Intelligence	Niceness
Experience	Giving	Intensity	Obedience
Expertise	Grace	Intimacy	Open-mindedness
Exploration	Gratefulness	Introversion	Openness
Expression	Gratitude	Intuition	Optimism
Extravagance	Goodness	Innovation	Opulence
Extroversion	Growth	Invention	Order
Exuberance	Guidance	Insight	Organization
Evolution	Happiness	Joy	Originality

Faithfulness	Harmony	Justice	Partnership
Fairness	Health	Grit	Progress
Faith	Heart	Kindness	Passion
Fame	Helpfulness	Knowledge	Peace
Fascination	Healing	Lavishness	Perception
Fashion	Holiness	Leadership	Perfection
Fearlessness	Honesty	Learning	Perseverance
Fidelity	Honor	Laughter	Persistence
Family	Hope	Liberty	Persuasion
Finesse	Hospitality	Liveliness	Philanthropy
Firmness	Humility	Logic	Patriotism
Fitness	Humor	Longevity	Playfulness
Flair	Intention	Love	Pleasantness
Flexibility	Imagination	Loyalty	Pleasure
Flow	Impact	Morals	Plenty
Fluidity	Impartiality	Mastery	Poise
Focus	Improvement	Maturity	Polish
Fortitude	Independence	Meekness	Popularity
Frankness	Individuality	Merit	Patience
Freedom	Ingenuity	Meticulousness	Power
Friendship	Inquisitiveness	Mindfulness	Practicality
Frugality	Influence	Moderation	Precision
Fun	Inspiration	Modesty	Prosperity
Goodwill	Instinct	Motivation	Preparation

PROSPER ON PURPOSE

Generosity	Integrity	Money	Privacy
Privacy	Results	Speed	Trust
Proactivity	Rules	Strategy	Tenacity
Proficiency	Responsiveness	Spirituality	Truth
Professionalism	Righteousness	Spontaneity	Tradition
Purpose	Steadfastness	Stability	Understanding
Prudence	Safety	Stillness	Uniqueness
Punctuality	Sacrifice	Strength	Unity
Purity	Satisfaction	Structure	Usefulness
Quality	Security	Substance	Validity
Quietness	Self-control	Success	Variety
Quickness	Selflessness	Sufficiency	Victory
Realism	Self-actualization	Support	Vigor
Readiness	Self-reliance	Supremacy	Virtue
Reason	Sensitivity	Surprise	Vision
Recognition	Sensuality	Stewardship	Vitality
Recreation	Serenity	Sympathy	Vivacity
Refinement	Service	Synergy	Warmth
Reflection	Sharing	Tolerance	Wellness
Relaxation	Significance	Tactfulness	Wealth
Reliability	Silence	Teamwork	Wholeness
Resilience	Silliness	Temperance	Wellbeing
Resolution	Simplicity	Thankfulness	Willingness
Relationships	Sincerity	Thoroughness	Winning

MELODY THOMPSON

Resourcefulness	Skillfulness	Thoughtfulness	Wisdom
Respect	Smartness	Thriftiness	Wit
Restfulness	Sophistication	Tidiness	Wonder
Restraint	Solidarity	Timeliness	Worth
Reverence	Status	Tradition	Work
Richness	Solitude	Tranquility	Zeal
Rigor	Soundness	Transcendence	Zest

Your Legacy

As you develop your values, think about how you want to be remembered. This is described as your legacy. Your legacy is how you want others to remember the work you have done in the world and what values you displayed in your life. Your legacy can also be described as what you will pass on to the next generation that will come after you. What do you want to hand down to others in your life? What do you want to be known for?

Activity: My Legacy

Using the following questions, describe what you want your legacy to be.

1. What values do you want to instill in others?
2. What do you want to teach others with your life?
3. What will others celebrate about you?
4. What impact do you want to make?
5. What might others say about you?

CHAPTER 4 - POSITION

You have been positioned where you are for a unique purpose, to solve problems and create a better life for those around you. You have been allowed to be born into the family, neighborhood and ethnicity you are a part of for a distinct and unique reason. It is on purpose and by design, because as part of your purpose, you are called to be connected to these people in some way.

Your Internal GPS

Your Internal GPS is the Global Positioning System that is within you. You know the way to go, you just have to tap into it. Your GPS will tell you where you are now and where you are going. Once you determine those coordinates, you will discover the way to get to your destination. Some of the ways you can tap into your Internal GPS are with quiet inner reflection, journaling, prayer, meditation, goal setting or visualization. Your Internal GPS is designed to redirect you when you get off course, and it will always reroute you to help you get back on the right path. Some key indications that you could be off course are experiences of rejection, failure, sadness, stagnation and frustration. When we are able to tap into our joy and inner peace, we will know that we are back on the right course again. Many times, the things that bring us the greatest joy tend to be in alignment with our purpose and help to get us back on track. We will explore your current position, which is where you are today, along with your destination which is where you want to be in the future.

Your Position in Life

There are three phases of your life where you have been positioned to connect with others:

1. Your Past – The places you have been
2. Your Present – The place where you are now
3. Your Future – The places you are going

There are several different positions you have held, and currently hold, in your life. You are positioned where you are for a reason. It is not a coincidence that you are there. Even if you have not enjoyed those places, you have been positioned there for a purpose. The positions you've be in are somehow connected to your purpose.

You may have a position in any one of these groups:

- Your family
- Your friends
- Your community
- Your school
- Your job
- Your age group
- Your ethnic group
- Your gender group

PROSPER ON PURPOSE

Everywhere you have been in life, there was something you were meant to give people while you were there and there was something you were supposed to receive while you were there. Maybe you were supposed to inspire someone, encourage someone or teach someone something. Perhaps you were there to learn a lesson from someone or develop a part of your character.

No matter what you have experienced in your life, it will all be used for a greater good, even if it did not feel good when you initially experienced it. We can learn how to turn all of our experiences into something good so that we can use it to help ourselves and others, as this is a part of discovering our purpose.

Experiences of Purpose

Throughout our lives, we have different experiences that help to develop who we will become. In each of the experiences, we have encountered people, events and lessons which offer clues to our purpose. These are your experiences of purpose.

Your experiences of purpose may include experiences you had in groups and communities you have participated in throughout your life where you have connected with others and held a particular position in those groups.

It may also include thoughts you've thought, emotions you've had or lessons you've learned. The impact you made or the things you learned in each of the experiences you've had in life may offer clues to your identity and your purpose.

People

The people you have encountered in your life are somehow connected to your purpose in life. Perhaps there is a pattern in the types of people you normally encounter. This is unique to you, because not everyone encounters these types of people.

What types of people have been attracted to you? Was it for a good reason or unhealthy reasons? What did you give to them? What have you learned from those relationships? What are you here to teach them? You were meant to encounter these people on purpose, and for a purpose. What do you believe that purpose is? What can you give them, or people like them, from what you have learned in your life?

Some of the people you may have encountered are:

- Family
- Friends
- Co-Workers
- Neighbors
- Classmates
- Strangers

Places

You have been many places in your life. Perhaps you have even been places to which you would rather not return. Everywhere you have been was for an important reason. Even the difficult places were designed to teach you something and allow you to encounter certain people and circumstances. The fact you were there creates a connection between you and those who have been there or are those who are there right now.

What have you learned from the places you have been? Why were you there? Did you give something to someone? No matter how pleasant or unpleasant the places you have been, you were meant to be there for a purpose. You may have to dig deep to discover that reason.

PROSPER ON PURPOSE

Some of the places you may have been in your life may have consisted of the following:

- Your schools
- Your neighborhood
- Your jobs

Profession

The professions you've had consist of the jobs you've held, the work you've done and the professional subjects you've studied in school. Why were you attracted to these things? Why did you choose those jobs? What occurred on those jobs? What did you learn that you can take with you? What did you enjoy or not enjoy about those jobs? How were those jobs in alignment, or not in alignment, with your personality, gifts and values?

Performance

Your performance consists of how well you have done in the things you have participated in and how well you have helped others. How well did you perform with that particular job, task, group of people? Were you able to influence them? Did you fail? What did you learn or take away from that experience?

Presence

Your presence is the way you impact those around you. Your presence can be felt even without saying a word. Many times your presence is speaking for you before you do. What impact have you made on people by simply being in their presence? Do you have a calming nature? Do you energize people? Do you inspire people? Do you intimidate people?

Reflect on the natural effect your presence has on others, even when you are not speaking. This can even include the effect you have on children, the elderly, plants or animals. What types of people are you drawn to? What types of people are drawn to you? How do people respond to you and interact with you? When you're not around, but your name is mentioned, what part of your presence is felt? Knowing how your presence affects people will help to determine how you should present yourself and manage your interactions with others.

Pain

Believe it or not, your pain has a purpose. In fact, your pain may actually lead you to your purpose. We often think of pain as a negative thing that comes to destroy us and rob us of something precious. However, we don't believe pain can be an indication of our strength. Often times we experience the most attacks in the areas in which we are actually strong, even if we don't feel strong in that area at the moment. If we never experience pain, we would not be forced to grow.

Some believe if we were strong in a particular area of our lives we wouldn't experience pain. However, when you are building muscles, you have to experience pain initially in order for your muscles to grow. It is a very unpleasant process but if you complete the growth process, you will find the pain subsides as you become stronger. What pains have made you stronger?

Pain can also be a great teacher. Pain in life teaches us patience and perseverance. When we learn patience, we are able to persevere in the midst of adversity. This allows us to get into position and enables us to walk in our purpose in order to become the answer to someone's problems. Pain in life teaches us lessons that perhaps comfort could never teach us. Your pain can become your platform to teach others what you have learned. What has your pain taught you? About life? About yourself? About others?

Perspective

Your perspective is the way you view things from your position in the world and it affects everything we see and do. Your perspective is unique and based on your identity and experiences. What is your perspective on various issues in your life? Did you have to overcome an old mindset in order to change your life? Do you see things differently than others do? If so, this is an advantage and a strength.

Play Your Position

The reason why you don't ever have to compare yourself or compete with anyone else is because you were uniquely designed and positioned exactly where you are supposed to be in the world. No one can occupy the unique position you hold. No one else can do what you do or do it how you do it. It is our job to discover our unique position in the world and evaluate where we have been, what we have done and who we have encountered in order to piece together the clues to our purpose.

In team sports, everyone cannot play the same position or the team as a whole would not win. In football, everyone may want to be the quarterback or the wide receiver, however if there were no offensive linemen the quarterback would not be able to make the pass. We may not like our current position and may desire to be in someone else's position.

However, when we are purpose driven we see the greater vision at work. We understand we are a part of something greater than ourselves and in order for it to be successful we have to play our position. When you connect your individual purpose with the greater overall purpose of the group you belong to, or the world at large, that is when you can accomplish greater work.

Sometimes we look around us and we see others that appear to be ahead of us in life. There are those who seem like they are always happy and successful. They always seem to be ahead of everyone else. They have the best jobs, relationships, house, car and life or so it seems. They always seem to come out first and we feel like we are last compared to them.

MELODY THOMPSON

In a race, one of the rules for runners on the race track is if you step into another person's lane while running, it automatically disqualifies you from winning. So, that means everything you did in that race doesn't count. Wouldn't that be disappointing? Imagine running a race and just stepping an inch into someone else's lane and all of a sudden you've lost!

We can empathize with the track runners' disappointment for such a careless error, however we don't realize that many people are making this same mistake in the race of life. There are many people who are looking in someone else's lane and looking at what their peers, neighbors, friends, family members or co-workers are doing. As a result, people disqualify themselves from the amazing goodness life already has in store for them.

Please remember, things are not always what they appear to be. No one's life is perfect. Expressing gratitude for what we currently have in our lives increases our joy and abundance, ultimately propelling us to move forward to achieve the things we want the most. You must realize, whatever you are designed to have in life, it belongs to you only. There is no competition or comparison for you, because you are unique. What is for you is for *you* and you alone. No one can touch it.

The only person you will ever compete with in life is yourself. You can only be better than you were yesterday. If we would just focus on becoming our best selves, we would never need to feel jealous of another person in life. When we are living our best lives, we have everything we want and need. You are in a class all by yourself. So, run your race and stay in your lane, because if you do, you are guaranteed to win!

You don't have to seem important in order to be impactful. You're here to play your part and do what you're here to do. That means you are not any more or any less important than anyone else. When you know who you are and become clear on your vision and goals in life, it makes it much easier to stay focused on what you are here to create and accomplish in life.

PROSPER ON PURPOSE

Self Discovery Questions

1. Where have I been positioned?
2. Who have I come in contact with in my life? What did they teach me?
3. What places have I been? What did I learn there?
4. Who am I positioned to help?
5. What professions have I had in my life? Which ones did you feel led to? What did I learn there?
6. How have I performed in the past? What have I learned from my experiences?
7. What affect does my presence have on others? How do others react or respond to me? Why?
8. What have my painful life experiences taught me?
9. What is my perspective on life? How is my perspective different than others?
10. What can I offer to others based on the positions I've held in my life?

Vision and Goals

Your vision consists of analyzing the current position of where you are now and then deciding where you want to be in the future. A vision statement provides a description of what you foresee as the optimal desired future state of your life and what you want to accomplish over a period of time.

Your vision statement should represent what you intend to see happen with your life, career, family, and other areas of your life, within one or more years from the current date as a result of you realizing your strengths and purpose. The vision statement defines the ideal end state of what you hope to achieve in the future. The statement should be inspirational, serving as the guiding compass for your life in the future.

Answer the following questions to develop your vision statement.

Questions to Define Your Vision Statement

- Who do you want to help?
- What do you want to see happen as a result of using your gifts and talents?
- What do you want your reputation to be in the next few years?

Vision Statements are future focused. Vision Statements focus on the result of the individual accomplishing their mission and goals.

A vision statement defines the *ideal end state* of what you *hope* to achieve in the future.

Motivations and Aspirations

Motivations are what give us the energy to start or continue doing something we have set out to do. When developing your vision, it is also important to understand your "why". Why are you pursuing those goals? Why do you want those things? What are your motivations?

You may have a desire to help others, or to continue the legacy of a family member. You may want to pursue your vision and goals to teach your children how to follow their dreams. Whatever your motivations are, it is a good idea to write them down and keep them in mind whenever the journey gets difficult. Remembering why you decided to pursue a particular path will help you continue on it, until you accomplish your goals.

Aspirations are things we strongly desire to attain in life. Aspirations are similar to goals, as these are the things we want to accomplish and feel will make us happy. Our aspirations can be a reflection of our identity and personality type. Not everyone wants the same things in life. Everyone has a different definition of success, happiness and fulfillment. Defining your aspirations will help you define your goals.

We can break aspirations into three categories: What you want to DO, who you want to BE and what you want to HAVE in life. On the next page, make a list of at least 10 things in each category.

MELODY THOMPSON

ASPIRATIONS		
DO	BE	HAVE

Self Discovery Questions

Vision

1. What do you want in life?

2. What do you *really* want in life?

(This second question allows you to challenge your answer to the first question. Ensure your vision is your own and in alignment with what you really want, not what society thinks is successful. For example to the first question you might answer, "I want to be a CEO of a Fortune 500 Corporation," because that sounds successful. However, in your heart you really want to run your own small business and work from home. Make sure your vision is in alignment with what you really want and not what may look good to others.)

Motivations

Why do you want this?

Wheel of Life

Your wheel of life consists of the 10 areas of your life where you would like to improve as well as maintain joy and balance. Below are some categories for the Wheel of Life. You may use the ones below or create your own.

1. Family – family, marriage, children
2. Friends – friends and social life
3. Fellowship – community, church, volunteering, organizations
4. Field of Work/Study – your career, business or school
5. Finances – your income, investments, retirement, giving
6. Fun – recreation, vacation

7. Fitness – your health and fitness
8. Faith – your spiritual life, your belief system
9. Future – future goals, planning
10. Fulfillment – personal growth and development

Wheel of Life

PROSPER ON PURPOSE

Circle your level of satisfaction with each of these areas of your life, from 0 (least satisfied) to 10 (most satisfied).

Family	0	1	2	3	4	5	6	7	8	9	10
Friends	0	1	2	3	4	5	6	7	8	9	10
Fellowship	0	1	2	3	4	5	6	7	8	9	10
Field of Work/Study	0	1	2	3	4	5	6	7	8	9	10
Finances	0	1	2	3	4	5	6	7	8	9	10
Fun	0	1	2	3	4	5	6	7	8	9	10
Fitness	0	1	2	3	4	5	6	7	8	9	10
Faith	0	1	2	3	4	5	6	7	8	9	10
Future	0	1	2	3	4	5	6	7	8	9	10
Fulfillment	0	1	2	3	4	5	6	7	8	9	10

Self Reflection Questions

1. Review your three highest and lowest scores. What led you to give those answers?
2. Which area do you feel is the most important to work on?
3. Which area do you feel the most motivated to work on?
4. Which area could see the most amount of improvement with the least amount of effort?

Your Ideal Life

Answer the questions for each area to describe your ideal life.

Family
1. What does your life look like in this area currently?
2. What is going well in this area?
3. What is missing in this area?
4. What would you like your life to look like in this area?
5. What can you do to improve in this area?
6. What is holding you back from improving in this area?
7. Is there a limiting belief that is holding you back here?
8. What resources can you find to help you in this area?

Friends
1. What does your life look like in this area currently?
2. What is going well in this area?
3. What is missing in this area?
4. What would you like your life to look like in this area?
5. What can you do to improve in this area?
6. What is holding you back from improving in this area?
7. Is there a limiting belief that is holding you back here?
8. What resources can you find to help you in this area?

PROSPER ON PURPOSE

Fellowship

1. What does your life look like in this area currently?
2. What is going well in this area?
3. What is missing in this area?
4. What would you like your life to look like in this area?
5. What can you do to improve in this area?
6. What is holding you back from improving in this area?
7. Is there a limiting belief that is holding you back here?
8. What resources can you find to help you in this area?

Field of Work

1. What does your life look like in this area currently?
2. What is going well in this area?
3. What is missing in this area?
4. What would you like your life to look like in this area?
5. What can you do to improve in this area?
6. What is holding you back from improving in this area?
7. Is there a limiting belief that is holding you back here?
8. What resources can you find to help you in this area?

Finances

1. What does your life look like in this area currently?
2. What is going well in this area?

3. What is missing in this area?
4. What would you like your life to look like in this area?
5. What can you do to improve in this area?
6. What is holding you back from improving in this area?
7. Is there a limiting belief that is holding you back here?
8. What resources can you find to help you in this area?

Fun

1. What does your life look like in this area currently?
2. What is going well in this area?
3. What is missing in this area?
4. What would you like your life to look like in this area?
5. What can you do to improve in this area?
6. What is holding you back from improving in this area?
7. Is there a limiting belief that is holding you back here?
8. What resources can you find to help you in this area?

Fitness

1. What does your life look like in this area currently?
2. What is going well in this area?
3. What is missing in this area?
4. What would you like your life to look like in this area?

5. What can you do to improve in this area?
6. What is holding you back from improving in this area?
7. Is there a limiting belief that is holding you back here?
8. What resources can you find to help you in this area?

Faith

1. What does your life look like in this area currently?
2. What is going well in this area?
3. What is missing in this area?
4. What would you like your life to look like in this area?
5. What can you do to improve in this area?
6. What is holding you back from improving in this area?
7. Is there a limiting belief that is holding you back here?
8. What resources can you find to help you in this area?

Future

1. What does your life look like in this area currently?
2. What is going well in this area?
3. What is missing in this area?
4. What would you like your life to look like in this area?
5. What can you do to improve in this area?
6. What is holding you back from improving in this area?

7. Is there a limiting belief that is holding you back here?

8. What resources can you find to help you in this area?

Fulfillment

1. What does your life look like in this area currently?

2. What is going well in this area?

3. What is missing in this area?

4. What would you like your life to look like in this area?

5. What can you do to improve in this area?

6. What is holding you back from improving in this area?

7. Is there a limiting belief that is holding you back here?

8. What resources can you find to help you in this area?

CHAPTER 5 – POWER

Every person possesses a measure of power within themselves. Power can be defined as the possession of control, authority or influence over a person, an object or even oneself. Your personal power is your freedom, right and ability to make choices in your life. Every human being is born free and possesses free will, however people and circumstances can try to take those rights away from us in life. You are powerful in your own right. Even if you have been victimized in the past, you have the authority to take back your power and not allow others to imprison your soul. When you value yourself, everyone around you will do the same. It all begins with you.

You never have to ask anyone for your power back, because they never had it in the first place. You already own it, you just have to take hold of it. In order to operate in your purpose, you need to know the source of your power and maintain it in order to reach your destination. If your power is depleted or spent in the wrong places it will be difficult to go where you are destined to go. Destiny and purpose require power in order to move forward. Perhaps not owning your personal power has kept you stuck in life. The good news is you have the power to change your course and move in the right direction.

The Importance of Power

We all have power. However, we can actually forfeit our freedom and power by giving it to others. When we look outside of ourselves to find what we need, we give our power away. Also, when we don't take responsibility for our own lives, we are essentially giving our power away to our personal circumstances, believing it is out of our control. When we believe others are more powerful than we are, we are telling ourselves we don't have the ability to make choices or changes in our own lives.

> *" Stop allowing anyone or anything to control, limit, repress, or discourage you from being your true self! Today is YOURS to shape*
> *– own it –*
> *break free from people and things that poison or dilute your spirit."*
>
> *– Steve Maraboli*

Reasons for Feeling Powerless

Often in our lives, we have experiences that make us feel we have no power. When we continue to experience these events, they create the belief that we are powerless to change things in our lives, or powerless to prevent people or situations from hurting us. When we believe we are hopeless, we learn to give up and to let our boundaries down. When our walls are down, we find it difficult to defend ourselves or to respond to situations that violate our lives in some way. These situations reinforce the belief that we are powerless, which causes us to feel stuck and unable to move forward.

PROSPER ON PURPOSE

In order to be powerful, or full of power, you have to learn how to harness your own personal power. It is difficult harness power if we give it away to everyone else. When we give in to others or esteem others more highly than ourselves, we can find ourselves giving our power away to those who may or may not use it properly. When we learn to build ourselves up and maintain healthy boundaries, we will discover and lay hold of the power that has existed deep within us all along.

A Few Examples of Situations That Condition People to Feel Powerless:

- Bullying
- Harassment
- Manipulation
- Domination
- Oppression
- Rejection
- Abuse
- Discrimination
- Abandonment
- Neglect
- Prejudice
- Humiliation
- Physical Harm
- Theft
- Loss
- Failure
- Injustice
- Peer Pressure
- Guilt Trips
- Poverty
- Underestimation
- Marginalization

Taking Our Power Back - Self Empowerment

Personal Power

Although life may convince us we are powerless at times, we actually possess an incredible amount of personal power. We must learn to rebuild our walls and take back our power in order to move forward and get unstuck. We will explore some techniques to reclaim your personal power and build your boundaries. One of the ways to empower yourself is to know your rights.

You have the right to:

- be treated fairly
- be spoken to respectfully
- have personal time and space
- disagree with someone
- do/not do something
- go/not go somewhere
- not give your money to someone
- keep personal information private
- say what you want/don't want
- make your own choices

> ❦ A lack of boundaries invites a lack of respect. ❧

Knowing your rights is not about being defiant, rebellious or irresponsible in our behavior. There will be times you may have to do things you don't want to do or make sacrifices for others. Owning your power is all about knowing who you are and what you want in life, without allowing others to pressure you into doing things that go against your

PROSPER ON PURPOSE

personal beliefs and values. Please know that it is important to help those around us but we do not have to allow them to abuse us physically, emotionally, mentally, spiritually or financially.

View the list of "Your Personal Rights" on the next few pages to review what rights you have as an individual. Feel free to add your own to this list.

MELODY THOMPSON

YOUR PERSONAL RIGHTS

I have the right to be treated with dignity and respect

I have the right to take care of myself and put myself first when necessary

I have the right to have personal time and personal space

I have the right to have my own thoughts and opinions

I have the right to respectfully disagree with the thoughts/opinions of others

I have the right to do what I want to do with my life

I have the right and the freedom to go where I want

I have the right to say I don't want to go somewhere

I have the right to not do something if I choose not to do so

I have the right to spend my money the way I choose

I have the right to not help someone if I choose not to do so

I have the right to not carry the burdens of others

I have the right to change my mind

I have the right to not know the answers and even to say "I don't know" or "I don't understand"

I have the right to say "No"

I have the right to take my time to heal emotionally, mentally or physically

I have the right to ask questions

I have the right to make my own mistakes in life

I have the right to ask for what I want in life

I have the right to pursue my own dreams and goals in life

I have the right to keep my personal information private

PROSPER ON PURPOSE

I have the right to feel and express my emotions

I have the right to be happy in life, even when those around me are not

I have the right to be successful in life

I have the right to be loved and appreciated, and to show the same to others

I have the right to be imperfect and perform imperfectly

I have the right to determine what my priorities are

I have the right to rest, relax and recuperate when needed

I have the right to be myself

I have the right to not be responsible for other people's thoughts, feelings, actions or problems

I have the right to not be responsible for making others happy or successful

I have the right to not be superwoman/superman

I have the right to ask for help

I have the right to receive mercy, forgiveness, empathy and understanding and also give it to others

I have the right to feel safe and protected

I have the right to feel upset when I have been wronged

I have the right to stand up for myself and my rights

I have the right to choose the people I want or don't want in my life

I have the right to _____

I have the right to _____

You have the right to exercise any of these rights, without explaining, apologizing or feeling guilty.

Boundaries

Personal boundaries are guidelines that you set for yourself about how others should treat you and behave around you. When we do not have clear boundaries in our lives, it can decrease our energy and our sense of personal power. Your personal boundaries are developed by many factors in your life, including your beliefs, attitudes, past experiences and lessons you've learned from social interactions.

Personal boundaries may be based on physical, mental, material, spiritual and emotional aspects, all of which may affect your self-esteem. Your boundaries may involve protecting yourself from harm, either mental, emotional or physical. When a person in your life steps over those boundaries, you respond in a certain way. You may respond with anger or surprise. Or, you might ignore the offense and think it over at a later time, wishing you handled it differently.

Many people have rigid boundaries which make them somewhat difficult to get to know, while others have almost invisible boundaries which make them susceptible to abuse or manipulation. You may have personal boundaries that you've set in your working relationships, personal relationships or in interactions with people you meet for the first time. There are some individuals who are narcissists who may not recognize the boundaries of others and feel that people are simply extensions of their own personality. It is important to develop boundaries to manage all types of relationships and personalities you may encounter in your life.

There are several types of personal boundaries which you might set for yourself. They include:

- *Physical* – These boundaries involve your personal space and dictate how you relate to the people or things around you. For example, some individuals may be more apt to hug while others may prefer to shake hands. When someone or something invades your physical space, you may react a certain way because of the physical boundaries you've set for yourself.

- *Mental* – Boundaries which apply to your personal opinions and values make up your mental boundaries. Standing up for what you believe in is part of the mental boundaries you set for yourself. Being open-minded when listening to someone else's contrary opinion, without responding in anger, is a sign that you've set healthy mental boundaries for yourself. Those who follow others without thinking and are mentally suggestible tend to have weak mental and emotional boundaries and can be swept into situations that are potentially harmful.

- *Material* – How you feel about giving things away or lending your personal items to others make up the material boundaries you set for yourself. You may not mind lending a book to someone, but when it comes to your money, you may disagree. Part of your material boundaries may be the expectations you have when you give or loan someone money or objects.

- *Spiritual* – Your beliefs concerning spiritual matters make up your spiritual boundaries. Some people try to manipulate the spiritual beliefs of others with persecution or with judgmental comments. If spiritual boundaries are important to you, you'll respectfully stand up for your convictions and decide how you react to others when they question or interact with you about your beliefs.

- *Emotional* – Healthy emotional boundaries involve accepting responsibility for yourself and your actions. Emotional boundaries protect you from feeling guilty about taking on the burdens of others. When you set up healthy emotional boundaries, you know your limitations. Negative comments from others aren't taken personally when you've set good emotional boundaries.

All of these boundaries represent the various types of limits you can set, which will determine your level of personal peace and power. If these boundaries are not respected, it may represent an opportunity to speak up for yourself.

Reasons for Setting Boundaries

Your comfort level and the way you respond to others all factor into the personal boundaries you have set for yourself. Without boundaries, it may be difficult to function because you may find yourself subjected to people who may try to manipulate or take advantage of you. When you decide to change your personal boundaries by making them stronger, know that you may experience some confusion and resistance from others.

Here are some main signs you may need to change or set personal boundaries:

- *You have difficulty saying "No."* Developing this type of boundary seeks to protect your inner peace and personal time. You may have a desire to please others and end up taking on tasks which eventually interfere with what you really want or need to do in your life.

- *Feeling powerless.* You may feel as if you have no power over your life because of the demands your children, spouses, family members and co-workers may make on your time. They may cross boundaries of respect and leave you feeling as though you've lost touch with your own wants and needs.

- *Your boundaries may be too rigid.* Perhaps you've set boundaries so strict for yourself that you've created a wall that no one can penetrate, either physically or emotionally. Rigid boundaries are good in some situations with certain people, but you may need to lower the wall for the right relationships to flourish in your life.

- *You feel that no one respects you.* If you feel that you're not receiving respect from others, including those close to you and those you meet for the first time, it's time to set appropriate boundaries and require respect.

- *Feeling resentful or victimized.* Continuing a relationship or situation where you feel resentful or victimized is bad for your health. You may need to learn how to deal with setting boundaries and communicating your desires, which will teach others how to treat you. You may even need to examine if this relationship should continue in this way.

- *You feel unsure of how to define your boundaries.* You may react one way with a certain situation and an entirely different way for another. If you're wavering back and forth with your boundaries, you may have more difficulty in teaching others just what your limits are.

Setting boundaries in your life is important to help you establish productive relationships, so that others will know your limits. Even with children, although you may love your children unconditionally, you must set boundaries with them as well so they may learn they cannot take advantage of certain people or situations.

When it comes to setting boundaries in our lives, Dr. Phil McGraw said it best in his book, *Life Code: New Rules for the Real World:*

> "My spiritual upbringing taught me to pray for the misguided people in my life, and I always have and I always will, and I hope you do the same for those in your life. But (and this is a big but) praying for them does not mean that we – you and I – shouldn't also

protect ourselves and those we love from them. In fact, it's our duty to self protect because, true to their reptilian nature, these people, like snakes, will inject their venom into us (if not destroy us) without flinching. We must open our eyes to the "games" they play and boldly confront this very negative and unsavory part of our world."

We want to treat everyone with kindness, however we don't have to allow them to negatively affect our lives.

Creating Healthy Boundaries

The LEADERS Method™ is a model I developed to help individuals create healthy boundaries and make assertive decisions. This tool will walk you step by step through the process of responding to requests made by people in your life.

The LEADERS Method™ for Creating Healthy Boundaries

Here are the steps in the process:

1. ***Listen to the Request*** – When someone makes a request of us, it is kind to listen to the request. There are times when we can feel frustrated with someone because they make constant requests of us, and we refuse to speak to them or listen to them. This can make them feel as though we don't care about them. It demonstrates a sense of respect and kindness to listen to others as they make their request. Don't cut them off or interrupt, hear them out and allow them to communicate their request.

2. ***Empathize with the Situation*** – Once we have heard their request, now we can offer empathy for their situation. We want to show that we care about the person and their request, even if it may serve as an imposition in our lives. Showing empathy is a great way to help the person know we've heard them and we understand the situation. Depending on the situation,

you could say something such as, "Thank you for letting me know about this" or "I'm sorry to hear you are going through that".

3. *Assess the Situation* – Now that you have understood the request, you must make an assessment of the situation. You can do this by asking more questions. Find out more details about the situation and make sure you are clear on all of the circumstances surrounding it. After you have asked all of your questions, now it is time for you to start making your own assessment of what the situation entails and what you are willing to do and what the other person will be required to do. You don't have to say yes. In fact, it is best to hold off on saying yes until you have thought it through and the rest of the steps have been completed.

4. *Determine Options* – At this point, you have a good assessment of the situation and can begin determining options. You can do this alone, without the other person being present. You may say something like, "Thank you for letting me know about this. Let me think about it and get back to you." This gives you time to think and develop options. Now, you will start to write down options for this situation. The options don't have to include the ones the other person has presented to you. You want to come up with alternative options, including ones that require the other person to take accountability for their situation. You don't have to be the hero.

5. *Evaluate a Course of Action* – Now that you have written down all of the options, this is where you will evaluate the consequences of each option. In this step, you will weigh your options and evaluate them before they are finalized or presented to the other person. It is fine to create a mutually beneficial situation, if possible. However, if that is not possible, it is most important for you to choose the option that works best for you. You do not have to hurt yourself to help someone else.

6. *Respond to the Request* – In this step you will respond to the request. You can present your final decision to the individual, or if you have both made the decision together, you can decide how you will move forward.

7. Stick to Your Position – Now that you have presented your final decision, the key is to stick to it. The other person may not like the decision that was made, and may try to persuade you to change your mind. If you have put much thought and consideration into your answer, do not feel the need to change it because of the other person's disapproval. If it is something that can be worked out to better benefit both parties, that is understandable and can be adjusted. However, don't feel a need to give into disapproval, guilt trips, temper tantrums, ultimatums or threats. These are designed to force you to change your mind once a decision has been made. Don't give in to these tactics. Remember to do what you said, be consistent and stick to your position. It may be difficult at first, but it will help you to gain respect in the long run.

The LEADERS Method™ for Creating Healthy Boundaries

L isten to the Request

E mpathize with the Situation

A ssess the Situation

D etermine Options

E valuate a Course of Action

R espond to the Request

S tick to Your Position

PROSPER ON PURPOSE
Making Empowered Decisions

Making empowered decisions does not come easy for everyone. We may have to work at the trait of being able to effectively express our wants and needs. Sometimes we may not feel like making a decision or expressing our desires, but it is important to do so in order to maintain healthy relationships and to care for ourselves. If you have not done so in the past, it may be time now to voice your opinion in an empowered way.

The outcomes of your empowered decisions may not always be what you want, but it will put you in control of your own life. More often than not, the outcome will be positive and your self-esteem and personal power will improve dramatically over time because of it.

First, we have to change our minds about how "powerless" we feel and begin to change the negative beliefs which have been instilled in our minds that keep us from acting from an empowered place within ourselves.

Here are some tips that might help with making empowered decisions:

- *Know your limits.* There are certain behavior patterns which you may consider permissible and some that just won't work for you. Determining these boundaries help you decide how far you will allow people to push you before you take a stand.

- *Let people know your mindset.* Speak up if someone pushes past the boundaries you've set. You can't expect others to know what you believe or are thinking, so you have to express yourself. Otherwise, you may be unhappy with the relationship in the future.

- *Assume responsibility for your own words and actions.* If you let problems go on in a relationship, you'll create an unhappy environment. Your problems are your responsibility and you must take action and not expect others to "fix" them for you.

- *Others people's problems are not your problem.* You can only solve your own problems and begin to make changes to express your personal ideas and beliefs. Don't worry about what others think and believe. There may be consequences when you do begin to assert yourself, but it's better than the stress and anxiety you'll feel if you don't speak up.

- *Be patient with yourself.* It takes time to become the assertive and confident person you want to be. You'll experience times where you feel you have let yourself down – and times when you feel happy because your self-esteem suddenly rises due to having good boundaries. Be patient.

As you progress on your journey to become more assertive, you will find that you're better able to cope with various situations which may come your way. You will also improve your communication skills with others, from co-workers to family members.

Assertive Decisions Empower You

Assertiveness is the ability to practice effective communication skills, which help you to stand up for yourself, while it also allows others the right to express their own opinions and beliefs. Assertiveness allows you to express yourself, which helps others to understand your position.

You may have a difficult time saying, "No," in certain areas of your life and may end up feeling angry and resentful of others if you believe they have taken advantage of you in a particular situation. Taking a more assertive stance will allow you to

"Deal with yourself as an individual worthy of respect and make everyone else deal with you the same way."

–Nikki Giovanni

communicate in a greater capacity and help you enjoy life from a more empowered state of being. Since assertiveness is based on mutual respect, it's an effective way to interact with others and to resolve conflicts which may arise in relationships.

When you allow yourself to become passive in certain areas of life, you give others an opportunity to take advantage of you and manipulate you into doing things you may not want to do. For example, if your co-worker asks you to take on another project that you don't have time for, you may say yes out of a need to please. Later, you're faced with long evenings of overtime and weekends that you don't get to spend with your family. A decision on your part to say no to the project would keep your mental and emotional health in a much more positive state, especially if you can offer a solution to the need for someone to take on the project. When we stand up for ourselves, we empower ourselves.

If you have been passive or felt powerless for a long period of time, you may notice some resistance from others when you begin to make assertive decisions. Many people you interact with may be accustomed to seeing you respond in a passive way. It may take some time for them to get used to the new you.

When it comes to developing the skills you need to be assertive with family and friends, remember the following tips:

- *Learn to say "No."* Being assertive with family and friends is sometimes more difficult than being assertive at work. Naturally, family bonds are much stronger than workplace associates, so it may be more difficult to find the courage to say, "No." However, it is possible.
- *Be clear with your requests.* Don't apologize or be unclear about your intentions when speaking with others. Use language that is clear and direct, which gets to the point and leaves no doubt of your request. For example, if you're asked at the last minute to do something that leaves

you pressed for time, be clear that you would need more notice before you could respond to the request.

- *Tell them how you feel.* If others don't know how you feel, they may continue to treat you the same as always. When you let others know how you feel, they may respect the fact you were honest and forthright enough to express your thoughts and feelings in a calm and assertive manner. Be clear in how you want the relationship to look in your interactions with them. Make sure to express yourself in a calm and controlled manner so your message is heard clearly, and not your emotions.

- *Rehearse the conversation.* Just as you would with co-workers, rehearse the conversation you'll have with friends and loved ones. You can practice beforehand in front of a mirror, or with another person. Practice assertive body language and be sure to look them in the eye when speaking. Again, cool, calm and controlled communication works bests.

- *Don't elaborate on your requests.* Sometimes, the less you say, the better. Avoid accusatory words and statements that begin with "you", which may change the entire dynamics of the conversation and make others feel defensive.

You can succeed in your personal relationships when you approach the situation with courage and consideration.

Developing an Empowered Mindset

An empowered mindset to deal with relationships in our lives means we must feel self-confident about our ability to speak up and solve the problems without feeling guilty or apologetic.

Developing an empowered mindset begins with knowing who you are and appreciating the value you bring to relationships. When you have this understanding, you will be able to feel empowered to be more assertive around family, friends and even co-workers.

Here are some techniques you can use to develop an empowered mindset that will lead you to more fulfilling relationships with those around you:

- *Use "I" statements* – When communicating effectively with friends and family, begin sentences with "I feel", "I need", "I would like" or "I want." For example, "When you speak to me that way, I feel disrespected. I would like for you to speak to me in a respectful manner." This will convey the message that you're aware of the other person's actions and how it makes you feel, while also stating the desired outcome and change you would like the other person to make.

- *Acknowledge when someone ignores your needs* – For example, if it bothers you that your friend is constantly late when meeting you for lunch, you can say, "This is the third time in a row I've missed my lunch break, due to you arriving late. In the future, if you are late, I will have to reschedule our lunch date."

- *Understand the person's dilemma* – When you express understanding, you're being empathetic with the other person and have a better chance of connecting with him or her. For example, if a person is asking for a loan and you don't want to (or can't) loan him money, you can say, "I understand you're going through a tough time, but unfortunately I can't loan you the money right now. I would be happy to sit down with you and help you to figure out a solution to your financial situation."

- *Disagree when needed* – Acting assertively in a disagreement means that you're fair and empathetic, but self-assured in your disagreement. Avoid bullying or intimidating the other person with whom you disagree.

Always being available for your loved ones has the potential to be physically and emotionally draining, depending on their needs. You need to practice taking care of yourself so you are able to maintain healthy relationships without losing yourself in the process of caring for others. When you can use these techniques to become more assertive with others, you will foster effective communication, gain the respect you deserve, build your self-confidence as well as empower yourself and others.

One word of caution: If you're dealing with someone who could potentially become violent or physically abusive as a result of you asserting yourself and you believe your life could be in danger, you may want to use your own discretion and speak to a professional first (doctor, psychologist, therapist, counselor or law enforcement officer) before asserting yourself.

ARISE Method™ for Empowerment

Sometimes we can take power from others without knowing it. When people are looking for our help, the most important thing we want to ensure is that we empower them and not enable them. Enabling people involves making decisions for them, trying to fix them or doing what they should do for themselves. Empowering people consists of helping people to make decisions and take action for themselves.

Taking on other people's problems causes us stress and never truly helps the other person. You will find some people seem to constantly have a problem or frequently need something. This could be the result of them feeling powerless to change their situation, or not knowing how to solve problems in their lives. It may also be the result of a chronic situation that needs deeper attention. We have to learn to empower others to take responsibility for their own lives.

By learning to empower others, we are also empowering ourselves to be free from the burden of false responsibilities while becoming a catalyst for positive change in the lives of others. We can do this by helping people to think of alternative solutions to their problem, instead of them asking us to "fix it" for them. When we do this, we are teaching people to be self-sufficient instead of co-dependent. This is the beginning of empowerment.

One technique I developed to empower others is the ARISE Method™ for Empowerment. With this method, I teach how to empower others through accountability, resources, inspiration, solutions and encouragement. The goals is to teach people to arise and walk in their personal power. The ARISE Method™ for Empowerment allows us to help others take accountability for their choices and their actions, while also helping them to take control in the problem solving process.

Many individuals have not learned to problem solve for themselves in life. Perhaps they've always had a parent, teacher, manager or friend who told them what to do or solved their problems for them. In order for us to help individuals to be mature and whole in life, we must teach them to solve their own problems, make their own decisions and take responsibility for their actions. If we continue to take on their burdens, they will not fully develop into mature individuals. They will continue to seek co-dependent relationships, where the other person solves their problems for them. With this method, we seek to *empower* individuals and not *enable* them.

MELODY THOMPSON

ARISE Method™ of Empowerment

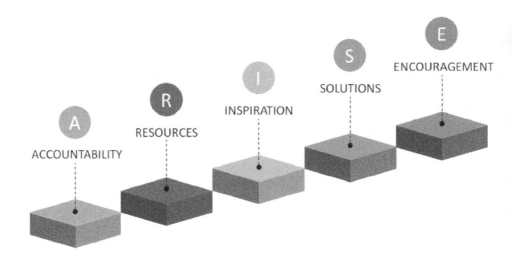

Accountability

- Hold people accountable for their actions
- Stop making excuses and tolerating poor choices
- Let people know this is their life and their choices

Resources

- Help them locate additional resources (besides you!)
- Connect them with others that are more equipped to help them
- Connect them with resources, people, counselors or support groups to help them

Inspiration

- Give them examples of what others have done to fix this same issue
- Show them examples of others who have made it out of their situation

- Support them and help them create positive affirmations

Solutions

- Help them brainstorm ideas
- Help them problem solve solutions
- Help them develop a plan and a timeline

Encouragement

- Encourage them to see they are capable
- Help them to see their potential
- Help them to be accountable

Questions to Ask Yourself

- Do I have the experience to handle this request?
- Do I have the energy to handle this request?
- Do I have the empathy to handle this request?
- Do I have the resources to handle this request?
- Am I acting from an empowered place?
- Am I empowering or enabling the person by helping them?

Self Reflection Questions:

- What ways have you been enabling to others?
- How has this helped them or hurt them?

- What can you do to empower yourself?
- What can you do to empower others?

Affirmations

- I exist and I am whole all by myself.
- I don't have to decrease so you can increase.
- I don't have to hurt myself in order to help others.
- I am a separate individual from you.
- I do not have to lose myself in you or your life.

Write 5 of your own affirmations to empower yourself.

The Results of Healthy Boundaries

When you learn to create healthy boundaries in your life, you will also experience a freedom that you may have never felt before, allowing you to move forward in your life with power and confidence. Assertiveness sets you free from the expectations of others and releases you to live a better life.

Eventually, as a result of becoming more assertive, your relationships will change and you will gain a new respect from others which you may not have experienced in the past. If you have been aggressive in the past, you will find people may now seek your advice and presence, rather than avoiding you. If you have been passive in the past, others may initially react in surprise, but in time they will have more respect for you.

Use the following checklist to assess your assertiveness as you progress:

- ☐ Are you expressing your opinions clearly and with confidence?
- ☐ Can you walk into a room and introduce yourself to those you don't know?
- ☐ Do you speak up when someone disrespects your values?
- ☐ Can you say "no" without feeling guilty or apologetic?
- ☐ Do you still let things build up in your mind and then lash out?
- ☐ Can you ask for help without feeling as if you're imposing?
- ☐ Do you speak your mind calmly during an argument or disagreement?
- ☐ Can you maintain eye contact with others?
- ☐ When you're pushed too far, can you express your feelings effectively?
- ☐ When someone is disturbing you, can you tell them to stop?

Personal Power

Our personal energy is a source of power in our lives. We all have a certain amount of energy. If we allow the wrong people and circumstances to sap our time and energy, we won't have enough needed for the important tasks in our lives. This is one way we remain stuck. We must evaluate the types of people and circumstances we are giving our energy to, and begin to make changes based on the impact these have on our power. Let's look at some of the things that may drain our energy and power.

Power Drainers

False Responsibilities

Oftentimes in life, we walk beside people to help them carry a burden that may appear too heavy for them to carry at the moment. Helping others in this way in itself is not necessarily harmful. However, when we begin to carry burdens that others should be carrying themselves, this is what causes us unnecessary pain. It is perfectly fine to help people, however if helping them ends up hurting us *and* them, we must look for an alternative solution.

When individuals refuse to take personal responsibility for their own lives, they place false burdens on us, making us feel guilty and manipulating us into doing what they want us to do. They can also make us feel like we are supposed to be their parent or their savior. All of these tactics are a violation of your boundaries and your free will. You have the right to say "No", without being the bad guy.

Toxic People and Places

Negative people and places are one of the biggest drains on our energy. The atmosphere in which you live or work is one of the greatest influences

PROSPER ON PURPOSE

on your personal peace, happiness and growth. If we allow toxic people into our environment, it threatens to deplete and contaminate our storage of joy and peace, which ultimately stifles our growth in life. We must learn to protect our personal space, in order to maintain our sense of well-being in life.

When dealing with toxic people, we must remember that people interact with us at the level of their own inner emotional health. We *re-act* to them at the level of *our own* inner emotional health. We must show mercy to others who may not yet have evolved to a state of being that allows them to act in a loving way toward themselves or others. They may have not yet gone through the healing or growth process. However, while we can be merciful to people in pain, we do not have to allow them to be in close proximity to us to repeatedly inflict the same pain upon us. We must allow ourselves the proper time and space to complete our process of healing, in order to be prepared to deal with hurting people. By working towards your own healing, it will inspire others to find their place of healing in life.

People Pleasing

When we feel a need to please people, we inadvertently end up giving away our power to others. We end up sacrificing our own wants and needs in order to gain the approval of others. These individuals may still not approve of us, which can create a never ending cycle of rejection, hurt and disappointment. When we feel a need to gain approval or love from someone else, we essentially are saying we are not enough on our own and we need their love and approval to be happy.

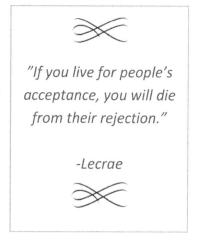

"If you live for people's acceptance, you will die from their rejection."

-Lecrae

This belief system can rob us of our

personal power and keep us stuck in life. If our actions are dependent upon the approval of others, it can limit our effectiveness and our ability to move forward in life. Not being able to say "no" to others can take a toll on your health, physically and emotionally. When we learn to love and approve of ourselves, we are able to remain confident regardless of what others think about us.

Perfectionism

Perfectionism can rob us of joy and energy, because we spend our time trying to achieve an unrealistic goal. Perfection does not exist, and the pursuit of it is an unfruitful venture. We often adopt habits of perfectionism due to learned behavior. We may believe we can escape judgment by doing everything perfectly. However, we cannot control whether or not people will judge (or misjudge) us. We also cannot control situations or outcomes to ensure they are perfect. We can only control ourselves.

Perfection in itself is an illusion and a mirage. When we try to chase that mirage, it appears to be forever elusive. The stress of trying to maintain perfection drains our energy and keeps us stuck, because it inhibits us from authentically connecting with others. When we operate from a place of perfection we are not our true selves.

Being human is all about making mistakes and hopefully learning from those mistakes. We can actually use imperfection as a motivating force for positive change. Even when we learn our lessons in life and make changes, we may still possess certain flaws and imperfections in our lives. However, the benefit is that through learning our lessons, we become better people, as opposed to perfect people.

When looking for perfection, we tend to compare people and things, noticing the differences between them. These perceived differences and categories allow us to then assess people and things as better or worse based on our perception. In reality, we are all the same. We all have the same ability to make mistakes, which demonstrates the commonality and humanity that we all share. When embracing our own flaws and imperfections, we are far more likely to forgive others and less likely to judge. The flaws in all of us allow us to relate to each other. In this way, our shared imperfections actually allow for positive interaction and relationship building.

Which is more appealing, a person who pretends to be perfect or a person who is able to admit their imperfections? The person who embraces their imperfections and owns them is far more relatable than the person who doesn't. Why is this? Well, most likely because we can relate far more to a person that reminds us of ourselves than to a person who doesn't. We know that we are all far from perfect. We have an innate sense of that imperfection. We also sense that we all share this tendency to try to cover our imperfections.

When you, as a person, let others see that you have flaws and make mistakes, you become more likable. Others will also trust you and what you say much more readily because of this admission. Eventually, you will be seen as much more authentic by exposing your flaws than by trying to cover them up with a mask of perfectionism. With that said, you don't have to expose every flaw. It is best to discuss the ones from which you have already learned and grown.

In addition, when you face the mistakes you've made and the failures you've experienced with a positive outlook, others are far more likely to attempt to face their own mistakes with optimism as well. Many people desperately try to hide any flaws they may have. They spend a lot of energy holding up the illusion of perfection. They do this because they have been taught that anything less than perfection is failure. Life can end up becoming miserable and lonely for people who live like this. Their days are filled with fear of failing and fear of getting caught making a mistake.

The process of striving for perfection steals our energy and takes the enjoyment out of our lives. When you are honest about your mistakes, you set an example that allows others to let go of the false illusion of perfection in favor of a rich and imperfect life, flaws and all. While you may not want to reveal all of your flaws and failures to everyone, as this would not be considered wise, it may be helpful to let others know you are human and have overcome obstacles just like everyone else. This helps us to connect with others as human beings.

The key to happiness does not exist in attaining perfection. Instead, true happiness comes from accepting who you are. In order to truly accept yourself, you have to be willing to also accept your imperfections. You need to honestly embrace those imperfections as an essential part of the real you. In order to accomplish this, you need to begin viewing your imperfections differently. You need to see them as things that make you unique, beautiful and strong.

You are a human being and like all human beings you are prone to make mistakes. You are no different than everybody else. Things get complicated. Life gets messy. Things need to be fixed after they get broken. It's all a part of life. Accept yourself as human and realize you are not perfect, and it's ok.

Negative Information

When we feed ourselves a constant diet of negative information and images, it can start to take a toll on our mind and emotions. We can begin to feel drained of energy, because we are trying to deal with what we have witnessed. There are plenty sources of negative information in our society. We must be discerning about how much of it we want to allow in our lives. Some sources of negative information could be news networks, social media, movies, television shows, gossipers and complainers. We have the power to decide which of these we allow in our lives. Whatever we look at and listen to the most, we eventually become.

Stress

We can feel stress from various situations in our lives, such as our jobs, families, finances, health, circumstances, or even world events. When we have excessive amounts of stress in our lives, it can negatively affect our physical health as well as our emotional and mental health. Stress has been labeled a silent killer and is often linked to ailments such as heart problems, pain, infertility, high blood pressure and even digestive issues. When we can simplify our lives and reduce the amount of stress we are exposed to, this will serve to improve our overall quality of life.

Clutter

When there is disorder or clutter in our personal space, it can cause us to feel cluttered in our thinking. This tends to drain our energy and leave us feeling unmotivated. When we are able to clear the clutter, then our productivity, creativity and energy also seem to increase.

Poor Diet & Health

Poor diet and health can drain our energy and impair our ability to maintain peak performance levels in our lives. When we are not taking care of our bodies properly, this can affect our moods, thoughts and emotions. Our bodies, minds and emotions require proper care and a healthy atmosphere in order to function properly.

Negative Emotions and Self Talk

Negative emotions actually affect our mental and physical health. Studies have shown there is a connection between our emotions and our bodies. When we are not at ease within our emotions, it can show up as physical symptoms or "dis-ease". Our own personal beliefs about ourselves can also affect our actions. If we believe we are incapable of achieving success, it may hinder our efforts to actually obtain it. We can challenge our beliefs and learn to create positive statements that will eventually help to frame our perspective in our lives.

You also have to work at eliminating all the negative behaviors that have been impacting your confidence and the way that you present yourself to the world. One way to do this is by keeping track on your inner self talk. This voice inside you head can very often be overwhelmingly negative. Be aware of these negative thoughts, but don't own them or give them any weight. Simply acknowledge them for what they are and replace them with positive truthful statements. Soon, you will find the negativity in your inner voice being replaced by a more positive and supportive voice that reflects the new way that you view yourself and your life.

Fear

Fear is an illusion and a shadow of the mysterious unknown. If we live in fear, we often create what we fear. We draw attention to our imperfections by being afraid someone will find them out and expose them to embarrass us. The things we fear somehow we self-destructively make happen for ourselves. The mind is an obedient servant. Whatever we think about long and hard enough with intense emotion will eventually come to pass because we will inadvertently make it happen. We do not necessarily do this on purpose, but naturally, since we tend to do or become whatever we believe.

Fear is an illusion and a shadow of the mysterious unknown.

Fear causes pandemonium and chaos. It causes us to attack others and attack ourselves. Fear only begets more fear. Our fearful thoughts, words and actions may be projected onto others, causing them to become fearful and keeping them in a box. When we are guarded and closed off, we are actually blocking and preventing ourselves from receiving what we need most, which is love and acceptance. Many times our fears are a result of fearful people projecting their fears onto us.

We can even carry generational fears, which are the fears and burdens of our family members, ancestors and predecessors. Ironically, we play out those fears, which is exactly what we don't want. Other people's fears can be masked as "concern" or "good intentions", however they don't understand they are acting out of fear and not love.

We can overcome fear with positive beliefs about ourselves and what can happen. We can also flip our fears, by believing the opposite is true. If fear says, "you're going to fail", then perhaps the opposite is true. Perhaps you will be incredibly successful. If you feel fear about not being prepared, then that could be a wake up call for you to get prepared, and once you do, the fear will fade.

Complaining

Complaining is the act of choosing to only focus on what is wrong and what we *don't* want, which can block our blessings. While we may desire a different outcome, due to the discomfort we may feel in our present condition, complaining keeps us stuck in the very place we don't want to be. It also blocks us from being able to see or receive the answer to our problem, as the act of complaining only sees problems.

It is equivalent to a hungry baby that wants to be fed, but he/she is cranky, fussy, crying and screaming at the top of their lungs. It is hard to feed this type of baby, because he/she is in such a state of turmoil, they can't receive the answer to the very thing they are crying about. When we are in a state of peace and calm, we are better able to receive all the resources we need to solve our problems.

MELODY THOMPSON

Failure

Fear of failure is one of the top fears most people have in life, which hinders many people from moving forward. The most successful people in the world are those who have failed several times in their lives, yet learned from their failures in order to achieve great success. Failure can actually be your greatest teacher and a stepping stone to success.

Failure can feel like it has knocked the wind out of our sails, leaving us feeling deflated and stuck. We can tend to believe that failure is an indication that some part of our identity, at the core of our being, is forever flawed. We tend to believe that because we failed, then that means we *are* a failure. However, this is an incorrect view of failure and of ourselves. Simply because you failed does not make you a failure. It makes you human.

We have to detach ourselves from outcomes. The truth is, we may fail at a particular task, but that does not make us a failure. The outcomes we experience in our lives are not a reflection of who we are. We do not control the outcome, we control ourselves. Separate yourself from the expectation of what the outcome should be. When we detach ourselves from the outcome, we can see it as an event and not part of our identity. In fact, we can see it as not only an event, but also an opportunity for growth and ultimately a pathway to success. As we allow our perceived failures to help us to grow in our character and in knowledge, we become a better version of ourselves, which ultimately leads to success.

Failure is actually a huge key to success. In order to learn in life, we must try different approaches and have different experiences. If we approach failures as opportunities to improve ourselves and grow, we can be on the path to success much quicker. Scientists approach failure much differently than the average person. Scientists try thousands of different formulas before they come up with a solution. Each attempt gives them insight and information about what works and what doesn't work. They use the data gathered from previous experiments to come up with another formula.

PROSPER ON PURPOSE

Eventually they are able to develop the right formula, through using different combinations gathered in their experiments.

We can approach our lives as a series of experiments. Although we may have been unsuccessful in our initial attempts, if we learn from our mistakes, we can eventually find the right formula for success. If we avoid trying in order to avoid failure, we prolong our path to success. We must realize, failure is not final, it is only feedback. You have to fail in order to succeed. You are not defined by your successes or your failures. You are defined by who you are within. You can find the fortunes in your failures if you dig deep and look for them. The pearls and gold nuggets you will find in your failures will set you up for huge success in the next chapter of your life.

Self Reflection Questions

1. How do you define failure?
2. How can you *redefine* your idea of failure?
3. What do you believe about yourself when you fail?
4. What do you believe about yourself when you succeed?
5. Are you a different person when you fail or succeed?
6. How many tries does it take for someone to become successful?
7. Name people who have failed and become successful later?
8. Do you believe your past dictates your future?
9. Can you recall a time when you feel like you failed?
    - Did you try your best?
    - Were you prepared?
    - Was it the right timing?

- What did you do well? What worked?
- What did you learn?
- What could you do better next time?

Power Builders

Confidence

Confidence is all about knowing yourself, trusting yourself and feeling good about who you are and what you are capable of doing. Certain people and experiences can build us up and leave us feeling like we can conquer the world. These events give us energy and encourage us. We also have the ability to build our own confidence and self esteem. Alternatively, there are situations that take our energy, deplete us and leave us weary. Spending time with the right people and in the right environments will help us to grow as we continue on our path to success.

Joy

The more joy you have, the more powerful you feel. When we are sad or depressed, it feels as though we have no energy to do anything. Joy can be explained as the delight, pleasure and exuberance one feels for life. The more joy we possess, the more strength and power we seem to have in life. In order to find more joy, we can surround ourselves with people, activities, images, sounds, scents and environments that foster a sense of happiness around us. It is important to find ways to cultivate and maintain our joy in life in order to be strong and resilient, even in difficult times.

Gratitude

When we express gratitude, we focus on what we have versus what we don't have. When we are grateful, we spend our energy focusing on the positive aspects of our lives. Gratitude expands our capacity to receive all the goodness life has to offer, because we are able to appreciate the beauty all around us. When we allow our minds to be in a state of peace and gratitude, we are more receptive to receiving the answers to the problems in our lives. Gratitude is one of the keys to helping us get unstuck in our lives. It causes abundance and solutions to flow in our lives, because we have proven to have the character and the capacity to appreciate them.

Positivity

Positive thinking has real power. It has the power to change your life for the better. It has the power to change the way you feel about yourself. It has the power to increase the confidence you have in yourself and to empower your entire outlook. The best part is that being positive is extremely easy to implement. All it takes to successfully implement a positive attitude is a bit of mental effort.

You have to look at every event that occurs during your day as an opportunity to be positive or to positively influence someone else. If you are not accustomed to being positive, this mental effort will feel awkward and uncomfortable at first. However, if you stick with it, it will soon become a habit. The positivity that you generate from this newly formed habit will influence how you feel about yourself. In other words as your positivity grows, so will your confidence.

Love

Love is most likely the number one need most people have, and yet many people feel they don't have enough of it in their lives. We can learn to love ourselves from within, which will in turn attract more love and loving people to us. We often feel we have to be a certain type of person in order to receive love, however real love is pure and does not require us to be perfect in order to receive love.

Love doesn't require you to prove anything to be worthy of love, you are worthy of love because you exist. Love doesn't require you to be perfect in order for you to receive love, love perfects you. Love doesn't require you to change in order to receive love, love changes you. Love doesn't require you to pursue it, love is in constant pursuit of you. Love doesn't require you to work to do anything to receive love, love works for you and it is given freely and lavishly.

Love isn't selfish; love always gives, in abundance, even when it is not reciprocated. Love doesn't take your life from you or require you to give your life to gain love, love gives you life. Love doesn't restrict, control or hold you back, love liberates you and sets you free. Love doesn't cry out for revenge when it has been wronged, love cries out for grace and mercy, even when it has been hurt. Love doesn't beat you down or put you down, love lifts you up, allowing you to arise and shine. Love does not hold grudges, love forgives always. Love does not despair or give up hope, love always hopes and always perseveres. Love is not impatient or demanding, love is patient and kind. Love is not finite or limited, love is infinite and eternal.

If I am not good to myself, how can I expect anyone else to be good to me?
-Maya Angelou

Love lives inside of us, if we will take the time to discover it and embrace it. When we discover that everything we need is already inside of us, we will stop searching outside of ourselves to gain what we already possess within. When we discover it, we can give it to the world around us.

Filling Your Own Cup

It is important for us to maintain self care. While we may have obligations and responsibilities in our lives that require our attention, it is important to care for ourselves in the process. If we don't care for ourselves properly, we won't be able to properly care for others in the long run. We can learn more about ourselves by spending time with ourselves and finding activities that we enjoy doing alone. We can get so wrapped up in spending time with others, that we forget who we are and what we enjoy. We have to learn to fill our own cup, because no one is responsible for ensuring our happiness and overall well being, except ourselves.

Living Your Best Life

Many people look at the lives of the rich and famous and they desire that kind of lifestyle. People long for a life where they feel important, pampered and well taken care of. We may long to look and feel beautiful, be well known and receive praise for our abilities. People believe the only way to have that kind of life is to become a celebrity. In their attempt to gain fame or fortunes, they make life decisions that may not be wise or beneficial, just to attain something that is already available to them. We all have the potential to be the star of our own lives.

Living your best life is all about recognizing the beauty and uniqueness within yourself, while taking care of yourself and maximizing your gifts and talents in a way that makes others notice you. When we learn to value ourselves at a deep level, we don't need to cry out for others to appreciate us or care for us. We learn to care for ourselves and praise ourselves for the beauty of who we truly are. When we learn to love ourselves, we start to shine from within. When we shine from within, we don't need a spotlight because we light up the room everywhere we go. We learn to enjoy our lives from a place of inner peace and wholeness, and this draws good things in our lives. This is true abundance and prosperity.

Don't limit your happiness to a certain dollar amount. Just because others may spend $50,000 on a vacation, doesn't mean you can't be happy with a $500 vacation. Just because others appear to be happy making $1,000,000 a year, doesn't mean you can't be happy making $50,000 a year. Money and fame do not equal happiness. Don't let the lack of money be a barrier to your happiness. If someone else has a million dollar home, it doesn't mean you have to have the same type of home in order to be happy. You may find happiness in a home that is a fraction of that price.

Find a way to get what you want that is feasible and realistic for you. This is how you will begin to live your best life. You will find you are much happier and feel more confident about yourself when you begin taking care of yourself without feeling the need to "keep up with the Joneses".

Also, make sure everything you want is because *you* want it, and not just because someone else has it. Jealousy causes people to want things that are not even good for them, simply because someone else has it. Discover what *you* like and what works well for *you*. By learning to be the star of your own life, you will empower yourself to find your own happiness and do it your way.

We are going to practice an activity called Live Your Best Life. We will answer the following questions in order to discover how to shine from within in our own lives.

ACTIVITY: Live Your Best Life

1. What person do you admire the most?
2. What aspects of their life do you admire and aspire to achieve for yourself?

If you were Living Your Best Life:

3. What types of things would you do?
4. How would you look?
5. How would you feel?
6. What would you give yourself?

PROSPER ON PURPOSE

7. How would you pamper yourself?

8. Where would you go? Restaurants? Vacations? Events?

9. What types of professionals would you have on your dream team?

10. Who would you have around you?

11. What talents would people praise you for?

12. What would people admire about you?

13. How would you give back to others?

14. What would you stop doing?

15. What is holding you back from doing some of these things now?

16. How can you implement some of these things into your life *now*, perhaps on a smaller scale?

Tolerances

What you condone will continue.

When we learn to tolerate circumstances in our lives that don't build us up, we find they seem to linger and continue in our lives. What we condone will continue. These hindrances can cause our energy, power and happiness to diminish. We may be tolerating our own unmet needs, household clutter, broken objects, crossed boundaries, frustrations, unfinished business, unfair situations, other people's poor behavior and even our own bad habits or beliefs that no longer serve us.

You may be tolerating more negative scenarios than you think. What are you tolerating in your life? On the next page, you will take a moment to evaluate the things you are tolerating and not confronting in your life. Once we become aware of what we are tolerating or allowing, this brings them into the forefront of our minds and eventually we will naturally start resolving these issues and changing our habits.

Tolerances	

Now that you have listed your tolerances, here are some questions to ask yourself in order to begin the process of resolving these issues:

Self Reflection Questions

1. What's not working in my life? What am I tolerating?
2. How can I improve this situation?
3. What resources do I need to help me?
4. What do others need from me?
5. What action steps can I take to get each of these situations to work the way I would like?
6. What habits do I need to change in order to improve these situations?

Lifestyle Modifications

We have a limited amount of time and energy, so it is best to examine our lifestyle to eliminate bad habits that hinder us from being productive and living our best lives. Productivity increases power.

Even when we know we have a bad habit in our lives, it may still be difficult to change it. We may lack the resources or motivation to change our habits, even if those habits are creating results we don't desire in our lives.

We may even have a goal we want to pursue, but feel stuck and unable to change our bad habits into ones that will help us to attain our goal. We will learn a technique, which we will call *Lifestyle Modification.* This technique will help us to connect with our internal motivations, find extra energy to tackle the tasks that seem difficult to begin and create new habits that benefit us and move us forward.

This process is based on the habit changing method discussed in Charles Duhigg's best-selling book, *The Power of Habit*. Habits are formed by a system that consists of a trigger, a routine and a reward. In his book, *The Power of Habit,* Charles Duhigg refers to the three steps of the "Habit Loop" as cues, routines and rewards.

In our examples, the steps are referred to as triggers, routines, substitutions and rewards. It is often difficult, if not impossible to change one's triggers or desire for reward. However, instead, while our triggers remain the same and we may seek the same reward, we can more readily and effectively change our routines.

We may not be able to completely eliminate certain bad habits, but we can replace them with new ones. Over time the old routine will be replaced by the new one and our bad habit will develop into more healthy habits.

MELODY THOMPSON

Lifestyle Modification Method

The process to change our lifestyle begins with recognizing what triggers the habit. When we are able to accurately identify our triggers, we can be more aware that we are slipping into a familiar routine. We can develop what are called cues, or reminders, to alert us that one of our triggers has been set off, and we are about to launch into a familiar routine. Fortunately for us, our routines are the part of the process that we can alter.

In order to begin the process of altering our routine, we must engage in the act of substitution. Substitution is the idea that we can replace our old negative behaviors with a new healthy behavior. For example, if our trigger is the feeling of sadness, and the routine we use to remedy it is excessive eating, the reward is temporary relief but the consequence is weight gain or potential health issues. We cannot stop the feeling of sadness from affecting us, but we can become more aware that we are feeling it. Being aware of this cue allows us to adopt a new routine.

With the new routine, instead of reaching for food upon feeling lonely, you might call a friend, a counselor or engage in another healthy activity. The result will be a much more positive outcome.

Steps in the Lifestyle Modification Process:

1. *Trigger:* An event that starts a particular habit or cycle. It is good to become aware of your triggers to avoid slipping into a negative cycle or behavior pattern.

2. *Routines:* The behavior or cycle that brings about a certain end result. This behavior can be positive or negative. This is the part that can be changed.

3. *Substitution:* Replacing old behaviors with a new healthy behavior.

4. *Reward:* The benefit you receive by engaging in these habits and behavior patterns.

PROSPER ON PURPOSE

Below is an example of developing a new routine, while keeping the same trigger and reward.

Old Morning Routine:

Trigger: Alarm clock rings

Old Routine:

1) I hit the snooze button 3 times, and go back to sleep.

2) I eventually get out of bed, because I have overslept and I am now in a rush.

3) I shower and throw on anything because I have no time to iron.

4) I rush out of the door with no breakfast.

Reward: I don't have to do much in the morning to get ready and I get a few extra minutes of sleep. However, I feel embarrassed about begin late and unprepared for my day.

New Morning Routine:

Trigger: Alarm clock rings

New Routine:

1) I get out of bed 1 hour early, to the sound of music on my new alarm clock, instead of a loud blaring alarm.

2) I make a yummy quick hot oatmeal breakfast with dried fruits and nuts.

3) I read and meditate on my day for about 30 minute before I take a shower and get ready.

Reward: I don't do much in the morning to get ready because I make sure I do my prep work the night before so I don't waste time in the morning. As a result, I also get a few more minutes of sleep. Now, I feel peaceful, calm and nourished in the morning, ready to go for the day. The yummy breakfast is also a reward. I feel good about being on time and prepared.

Night Routine: (done the night before, to prepare for the morning):

1) Prepare clothes and shoes to wear for the next morning.
2) Decide what quick food I'm going to make for breakfast and make sure the items are ready.
3) Determine what book I want to read in the morning, and have it ready.
4) I go to bed earlier so I can get enough sleep and not feel tired in the morning.

Lifestyle Modification Questions:

Routine

What is the bad habit you want to change?

What is your trigger, which makes you feel or act a certain way?

What is the routine or habit you engage in to respond to that feeling?

Where do you feel you learned to adopt this routine or habit?

Reflection

What is the positive benefit you receive from engaging in that habit or routine?

When you have completed this habit, what is the reward? How do you feel?

What does that behavior really get you?

What are the negative effects of this habit? How does it affect others?

What does this behavior allow you to avoid?

If you do not change this habit or routine, how would that affect you?

Reward

How will you celebrate when you reach your goal?

What is something you could reward yourself with once you complete your new routine?

What reward could you grant yourself once you begin practicing your new habit?

Replacement

How could you change your behavior or routine in order to get a positive result?

How can you achieve the same reward with a different routine or set of behaviors?

How can you become more aware of this trigger to be able to change your routine?

What kind of structure can you place around yourself to make sure you remember to change this behavior?

What routine will you do instead?

What is a positive affirmation you could develop to support your new routine?

Responsibility

What resources could help you to stay on track in your new routine?

Who could be an effective accountability partner to help you stay on task?

Lifestyle Modification Worksheet:

Describe a change you want to make to an old habit or routine. Write out the steps you will take to replace old habits with new ones.

Old Routine

Trigger:

Routine:

Reward:

New Routine

Trigger:

Routine:

Reward:

CHAPTER 6 – PURPOSE

Purpose is described as a person's sense of resolve or determination, or the reason for which something exists or is used. Most often, purpose is focused on what we can do for others. Purpose is connected to an assignment that is much bigger than we are. While passion may satisfy us, purpose may require a sacrifice from us. Purpose requires us to become greater in order to do greater work.

Many people confuse passion and purpose. While these may work together, they are very different from one another. Passion is described as a strong feeling, desire or intense emotion about something. Without passion, it is difficult to achieve any great purpose. However, purpose requires much more in addition to passion to be able to sustain the ups and downs of the journey.

Passion vs. Purpose

The difference between passion and purpose is passion may come and go, depending upon the circumstances. However, purpose requires us to see a bigger picture, become steadfast and commit to completing our assignment, no matter the cost or the circumstances. We know we are purpose driven when we feel our assignment is something that is in service to others and has a sacrificial element to it. With purpose, we may be required to let go of something we really wanted in order to fulfill a greater vision for our lives. It may require us to heal from past events, get more education, leave our current profession, let go of our insecurities or come out of our comfort zone. However, the rewards and benefits are always greater when we follow our purpose because the impact of purpose lasts longer and reaches further.

Many people believe they will feel an incredible amount of joy when they discover their purpose. While joy is an emotion that you may feel upon discovering your purpose, the discovery of your purpose may also illicit other feelings. When you discover your purpose you may feel it is bigger than you, which may initially cause feelings of fear, anxiety, unworthiness, and confusion about how it will all come to fruition. You may even be hesitant and feel as though it is something you don't want to do. You must be willing to count up the cost and realize no matter what your purpose may be, it will require work and surrender to complete it. When you begin to walk in your purpose, everything will make sense and you will feel a sense of fulfillment, satisfaction and joy knowing it was all worth it.

When you first start walking in your purpose, it may require you to work harder than you've ever worked in your life. You may experience opposition. You may have to deal with naysayers, haters, rivals. You may have to leave behind old habits, old ways of thinking, unfruitful relationships, dead-end jobs, toxic environments. You may have to give up certain behavior, people and places that stifle you and won't let you grow, in addition to false identities, insecurities and limiting beliefs that have kept you stuck. You may have to stretch and push yourself more than you ever have in your life. You have to get comfortable with possibly being misunderstood and even being isolated from others for a season. Not everyone makes it to their purpose because some may not willing to do the work and go through the process. It is similar to climbing a mountain. Not everyone makes it. You must be willing to go the distance to become your greatest self in order to achieve your purpose.

Myths About Purpose

There are many myths and misconceptions about what purpose is and how it fits into one's life. We will explore some myths and misconceptions about purpose and explore some truths and realities of what purpose means in life.

Myth: I only have one purpose and once I know my purpose it will never change.

Truth: Purpose is not a one-time event. There is a purpose for every season of our lives.

We are always serving some type of purpose in each season of our lives. It is our responsibility to determine the purpose for the season we are in. Just like seasons change, our purpose can also change and evolve with each phase of our lives. Our purpose just increases in scope and responsibility as we complete each assignment.

Depending upon how well we handle each assignment, we will be given another assignment of greater or lesser responsibility. It is important to not just learn the lessons in our lives, but to also pass the tests. We don't get promoted to the next level simply because we went through something, survived it and learned a lesson. We go to the next level because we learned the lesson, released the pain, developed a strategy, changed our habits and passed the test. If we past the tests, we go to the next level. If we don't, we either stay where we are or go back to learn the lesson all over again.

Myth: When I discover my purpose, I will be overjoyed about doing it.

Truth: Your purpose may require you to do something you may not want to do when you first discover it.

Pursuing your purpose may require you to do things you never desired to do. However, although it may not seem appealing to you at first, when you actually begin working on it, you will feel a knowing in your heart that this is what you are meant to do with your life. Over time, it will become easy and enjoyable.

Myth: My purpose will be something I absolutely love to do.

Truth: Your purpose may require you to give up something you love.

While there may be aspects of your purpose that you love, not every part of your purpose will be enjoyable, as it may require a sacrifice. You may have to make certain changes in your life in order to reach your purpose. When you do, you will find you become the best version of yourself and you will love what you are doing.

Myth: My friends and family will support me when I discover my purpose.

Truth: Your purpose may separate you and cause you to be misunderstood.

Not everyone will understand your purpose or the sacrifices you have to make in order to attain it. However, if you focus on your goal, in time everyone will see the results of your dedication and why you were so focused on your purpose.

PROSPER ON PURPOSE

Myth: My purpose will be something I feel totally qualified and prepared to do.

Truth: Your purpose may require you to do things you've never done before, and you may even initially feel unqualified to do it.

You may even have to obtain new education and training in order to fulfill this new assignment. This may be a sacrifice initially, however once you finish you will say it was all worth it in the end.

Myth: I will feel totally confident and comfortable in my purpose.

Truth: Your purpose may require you to step outside of your comfort zone.

You won't always want to step outside of your comfort zone, but when you do, you will step into a new dimension that you never knew existed. You will become greater than you ever imagined. You will see power that you never knew you had. You will do things you never thought you could do and you will experience miracles.

Potential side effects of not living in purpose

- Frequently changing jobs
- Lethargy/Apathy
- Feeling like a failure
- Sadness and depression
- Feeling confused
- Feeling lost
- Feeling worthless
- Feeling stuck
- Feeling unfulfilled
- Feeling jealous

A few things that hinder people from operating in their purpose

- Fear
- Unforgiveness
- Insecurity
- Anger
- Regret
- Jealousy
- Guilt
- Blame
- Entitlement
- People Pleasing
- Discouragement
- Unworthiness
- Running from Calling
- Timing
- Going through Process
- Laziness
- Poor Decisions
- Wrong Environment

Types of Purpose

There are different types of purpose and different seasons of purpose in your life. Your purpose changes at different times in your life. There are certain times when it feels our purpose is greater than others.

Different Types of Purpose

- Individual Purpose
- Marital Purpose
- Parental Purpose
- Family Purpose
- Seasonal Purpose
- Corporate Purpose
- Regional Purpose
- National Purpose
- Global Purpose
- Generational Purpose

PROSPER ON PURPOSE

The Phases of Purpose™

There are seven aspects to discovering your purpose, which I call the Phases of Purpose™. The Phases of Purpose™ are a series of phases one walks through in the purpose discovery journey.

The Phases of Purpose™ consist of:
1. The Awareness Phase
2. The Assignment Phase
3. The Assessment Phase
4. The Agreement Phase
5. The Adjustment Phase
6. The Acknowledgement Phase
7. The Appointment Phase

These phases are an important aspect of the purpose discovery process. We will explore each of them in more detail.

Awareness

In the awareness phase, you start to realize there has to be more to life than where you currently are. You begin to wonder what your purpose is and you begin searching for it. You realize you are meant to do and be something great in this world. You may begin to feel dissatisfied with your life, even if you have everything you thought you wanted. You may begin to engage in deep reflection, meditation, prayer and even seek out advice regarding your purpose. It is in this process that you may begin to receive clues or insight into what your purpose could be.

Assignment

Once you begin to seek information about your purpose, you may start to receive details about your assignment. Your assignment consists of the greater work or higher calling you are destined to fulfill. There is an assignment or purpose for every chapter of your life. Our assignment changes with each new phase of life.

Your assignment has three main components: *Audience, Announcement and Alignments.*

Audience

Your audience represents the people you are called to influence. When we understand our purpose or calling, it is important to also understand who we are called to help. Within our purpose, we have the ability and authority to influence a certain group of people. When we stay within this sphere of influence, we find people seem to receive us, listen to us and respect us. When we step outside of this sphere of influence, we may find some resistance or we may find that we have to work harder in order to be successful. Your audience may also be known are your target market, your niche, your sphere of influence, your territory or your domain.

When you understand your audience, you will find your domain. A domain is an area of knowledge, influence or expertise. Everywhere you have a domain, you have dominion. Dominion is the power to rule or have supreme authority. There is a place in this world where you have dominion, and it is attached to your experiences, knowledge and strengths. Everywhere you have dominion you are able to dominate.

To dominate is to have a commanding or prominent place or position in something; to have mastery, control, or preeminence. When you know your audience, your gifts will make room for you and how you can find success in areas where other people struggle. If you try to operate in

PROSPER ON PURPOSE

someone else's gift or domain, it won't work for you. You have to know what works for you.

Dominion includes:

- Influence
- Impact
- Information
- Innovation
- Inspiration
- Increase

Questions:

1. Who is my audience, my target market/niche or sphere of influence?
2. What group of people have you been successful working with?
3. What groups of people seem to receive, respect and listen to you?
4. What groups of people do you belong to?
5. What have you overcome?
6. Who could you help with your story of overcoming?
7. What have you been equipped and prepared to teach or give others?
8. Who needs the most help? Is there anyone currently helping them?
9. What group of people do you feel passionate about helping?
10. Are you assigned to a person, family, organization, group of people, a city, a region, a nation or several nations?

Announcement

Your announcement can be the message you are to deliver to your audience or the cause which you will represent. Your announcement is connected to your values and what you stand for. You could deliver your message through music, writing, speaking, visual art, design, or through operating in excellence in whatever field of endeavor you choose. Your announcement can even involve supporting or creating an organization that is in alignment with your values. You can be called to make a difference in the world individually or within an organization. You may feel a desire to align with charitable organizations, support a particular cause or become an advocate for certain justice issues. These are all examples of your announcement and how you can stand up for certain causes and become a voice in the world.

Questions:

1. What are your top 5 values?
2. What are the biggest lessons you can share with others?
3. What do you believe your message(s) is to others?
4. What do you want to represent in the world?
5. What causes do you want to support?
6. What have you learned in your life that you believe you are meant to teach others?
7. How can you use your voice and your influence to help others?

Alignments

Your alignments are the people and organizations with whom you will connect and align. These connections are people who may operate in front of you, beside you and even behind you. The people in front of you will be individuals such as mentors, teachers, managers, advisors, coaches, schools or organizations with which you may work. These connections and alignments are very important, because they have a hand in shaping your character. These individuals will help you advance in your development much faster than if you were learning all these lessons on your own. Not every mentor has to be someone with whom we have a personal

PROSPER ON PURPOSE

relationship. It can also consist of people we watch, admire and learn about from afar. We may watch their videos, read their books or listen to their podcasts. There are many ways to benefit from the teaching and wisdom of others who provide a wealth of knowledge and information that will benefit us in our work.

Those who work beside you may consist of peers, friends, family members, colleagues, associates and even joint venture partners. These are the individuals who would be considered your peers or partners and may even operate in the same field of work. These connections can be very valuable, because they can provide support, encouragement and even advancement in your specific industry. By making connections with the right professionals, oftentimes you can go further much faster with a team of people who are moving in the same direction you are. The key is to find people who are dedicated to the same or similar cause or have a similar mission, and are open to collaboration and not competition.

Those who work behind you are those who may be employees, mentees, interns, young people, your children or even individuals who look up to you for advice and wisdom. These relationships should be chosen *wisely* because they can require a good amount of time and energy to maintain. However, these relationships are important because once we have received information and wisdom from others in order to help us become successful, it is only right to pass along what we have received.

The mark of a great leader is someone who is interested in not only making themselves great, but also making others great. We must seek individuals we can train and mentor to pass on what we have learned and leave a legacy. If you don't pass on what you know, your purpose dies with you. When we teach what we have learned, we leave a lasting legacy that lives on inside of others. Legacy is not just what we leave to others, it's what we leave *in* them.

Assessment

In the next phase, the assessment phase, this is where you will determine if you are ready to pursue your purpose. You will take an assessment of the assignment to determine if you have what is required in order to complete the task. After you discover your assignment, you will then take an assessment of yourself, your skill set, your strengths, what is required to do the work, the people and resources needed to complete the assignment and the needs of the people you are called to help.

You may not feel qualified or equipped with any of those things at the beginning. You may have to make some sacrifices in order to obtain the necessary training and resources in order to complete your assignment. Once you start on the path to engaging in your assignment, you will find all of the resources needed to complete the task will come to you, including the confidence and energy you need.

When you assess yourself, you may need to confront, challenge, change or cut off some critical aspects of your life in order to pursue your purpose. When you confront your issues, you have an opportunity to change them. Once we begin the process of changing ourselves in order to become our best selves, we may even be challenged to cut off certain things in our lives. We may have to cut off bad habits, toxic people or old belief systems. Whatever we are required to change about ourselves, it will only be for our benefit and the fulfillment of our purpose to do so. Once we have chosen to make the appropriate changes, we can then develop a plan and course of action for how we will carry out our assignment.

Agreement

When you receive the full understanding of your purpose and assignment, and have completed your assessment, the next thing required is your agreement. Many people receive a glimpse of their purpose and the calling in their life, however they are not willing to pursue that purpose.

PROSPER ON PURPOSE

Perhaps they are not ready to give up their own plans. There are many people who "run" from their calling or their purpose. There are even those who feel unworthy and fearful and thus do not operate in their purpose. There are many reasons why people may not agree with their purpose. However, a crucial step in the pursuit of purpose is to accept and agree with what you understand your purpose to be, as it is revealed to you. The agreement and acceptance is similar to signing a contract. All it takes is a "yes" and the decision to move forward. Once you agree to start on this journey, that's when amazing things begin to happen in your life.

Adjustment

Once you are in agreement with your assignment and calling, you may now have to make adjustments to your identity and character. In order to go to a place you've never been to before, you will have to adopt new beliefs, new habits and new connections. You may even be required to physically move to a new place. You will be required to step outside of your comfort zone into the growth zone. This is a period of transition, where you become a new person. This is a difficult place because it requires stretching in all directions.

You will be stretched in your abilities, your work, your relationships, your character and your beliefs. This is an ascent, similar to as if you are climbing a mountain. This can also be known as the butterfly process, since in this phase you go from being a caterpillar to a butterfly. You go into a hiding phase, where people don't really see much of you but you are changing, preparing, working, transforming and becoming a new person. Everyone may not understand your transition during this phase.

In this phase, you are not able to take old baggage, bad habits, toxic relationships and old ways of doing things into your new season of life. You can't go higher with heavy weights. You will have to let go of things that were hindering you from becoming your best self. You will go through a pruning process. With everything you let go of, you become more fruitful and more productive. You are able to develop better habits, better relationships and a better circle of friends. You become a better version of yourself, which allows you to create your best work in the world and fulfill your purpose. As a result of this process, eventually you go from crawling to flying!

Acknowledgement

The acknowledgement phase is the point in your journey at which people begin to recognize your gifts, talents and expertise. People start to realize you are called to do something significant. Your greatness begins to show through your demonstration of your strengths and abilities. This is the point where you begin to become publicly acknowledged by others. Prior to this, you were relatively unknown, still building your skills and experience.

You may be extremely talented and operating in your purpose for years, however it seems you just don't get the kind of recognition you believe you deserve. This is because people have not yet acknowledged you. You have been hidden. You are hidden so you can learn to grow in your character and integrity. So, when you are in a place of leadership, you will not only be experienced in your craft, but also ethical, humble, kind, strong and prepared for the journey ahead.

While we may desire to be in a place of leadership or even to be recognized by others for our gifts and talents, it may not be our time yet. We may be hidden from others, until we have completed the process of development. Life takes us through a process to develop us into the person we were always meant to be. It may feel uncomfortable when others do not recognize our unique talents. However, if we learn our lessons at each stage of our lives, eventually we will come to a place where we are mature and prepared to be revealed to the world.

PROSPER ON PURPOSE

Everything beautiful grows in a hidden place. Seeds grow in dark places, hidden from others, buried by dirt. They experience darkness, isolation, rain, cold, extreme heat and even periods of drought. It is not until they break off their shell and push past the dirt that they can grow to their full potential and flourish in the light. The dirt and shade that others threw on you seemed like it was meant to bury you and break you. They didn't realize you were a seed with life hidden inside of you.

Seeds always produce something greater than what appears on the outside. So, the dirt and the dark place only help you to grow into who you were always destined to be. If you stayed a comfortable little seed, you would never discover you are really a beautiful flower or a tall oak tree. The adversity and obscurity develops your character, so you can shed the old shell and become your greatest self.

There is greatness in you! Don't try to elevate yourself or prove yourself to others. Stay hidden until it's time, so you can grow into your full potential. Be grateful for your hidden season, because it is your opportunity to learn, develop and grow as much as you can. When it's your time to step into the spotlight, you will be complete and whole, having learned all your lessons. The right people will recognize you at the right time. At that point, you will have something great to offer the world.

Although acknowledgement begins to happen in this phase, it does not mean we have yet arrived at our leadership position or place of destiny. While the acknowledgement is the beginning of people recognizing our abilities, it leads us into the appointment phase, which is the final phase of our purpose.

Appointment

Your appointment is the place of promotion, elevation and leadership that you have worked so long and hard to reach in your life. This is the time period when you are fully recognized and promoted into your purpose. Your appointment consists of a specific time and place when you are elevated to operate in the higher purpose for a particular area of your life. You may find yourself in a leadership position, in your dream career, a new business venture, a marriage or even becoming a parent.

When you are appointed, you are in a place of significance, prominence and leadership. Some people refer to this as being "your time" or "your shining moment". This is the place of your destiny, where you have been fully recognized by others and allowed to operate on a level of leadership that affects others. You have learned your lessons and passed your tests. This is where everything you have experienced in your life makes sense and serves to help you fulfill your higher purpose.

Defining Your Purpose

One of the best ways to define and describe your purpose is to develop your mission statement. Everyone has a mission, including individuals, families, businesses, government agencies, non-profits and corporations. In order to accurately understand your purpose, it is important to have a well developed mission statement. A mission statement will help you determine the direction for your life, family, career or organization.

Your mission statement can be a guiding statement that will help you make decisions about the activities in which you will and won't engage. It can prevent you from taking on responsibilities or engaging in activities that could potentially distract you from your main goals. A mission statement is a necessity in order to remain clear on your purpose and why you do what you do.

PROSPER ON PURPOSE

Your Mission Statement

The words mission and purpose are synonymous. In fact, in business, a mission statement can also be called a purpose statement. When we mention the term mission statement, most people think about a corporation. While many organizations do utilize a mission statement, mission statements can also be beneficial for individuals as well. Much like a corporate mission statement, your personal mission statement explains why you exist and what you are here to do. In short, your mission statement defines and explains your purpose.

Your mission statement is important to help you determine what you stand for and even what opportunities you will pursue. It sets the tone for the overall direction and path your life will take, by eliminating the ideas and opportunities that do not align with your purpose. Organizations and individuals both need a mission statement to provide direction about what they want to pursue and how they will make it happen. This is the framework from which your personal life strategies are formulated.

While a personal mission statement will incorporate your purpose, your vision and your values, it is different from a vision or a values statement. People often mix up the two terms – mission statement and vision statement. A vision statement is usually one sentence, or even just a few words that defines the end state of what you hope to achieve in the future. Your mission statement can be slightly longer, preferably just a few sentences at most. It provides more information about your purpose and what you do on a day to day basis.

Ultimately, your mission and vision statements should explain who you provide value to, how you provide this value, and what makes you unique. We will focus on developing your mission statement as a summary of your strengths, values, purpose and what you intend to offer to the world.

A mission statement should define why you exist, who you help, what you do and how you operate on a *daily basis*.

 A vision statement defines the ideal *end state* of what you *hope* to achieve in the *future*.

Mission Statement

A mission statement focuses on the present and provides a description of the purpose, values and reasons why the individual or organization is needed by others. A mission statement should define why the person or organization exists, who they help, what they do and how they operate.

It is a good practice to make the mission statement into one that can be memorized and articulated when needed. Your mission statement is helpful to use in formulating an elevator speech.

A good personal mission statement communicates your overall values and purpose, clearly identifies the skills you provide, identifies the industry you are in and briefly identifies your target market whom you help.

> Mission statements are present focused. Mission statements focus on solving a current problem, and describe the overall purpose of an individual.

PROSPER ON PURPOSE

Answer the following questions to develop your mission statement.

Questions to Define Your Mission Statement
- What products/services do you provide?
- What methods do you use to provide these products/services?
- Who is your audience?
- How do you help your audience?
- What makes your products/services unique?
- What are your values?

Developing Mission Statements

When developing your mission statement, you will describe: the gifts and talents you provide + who you're providing it for + the expected result.

For example: I use my passion and expertise in technology to inspire researchers to create medications to cure rare diseases.

Example Mission Statements:

Oprah Winfrey, Founder of OWN TV Network: *"To be a teacher, and to be known for inspiring my students to be more than they thought they could be."*

Amanda Steinberg, Founder of Dailyworth.com: *"To use my gifts of intelligence, charisma, and serial optimism to cultivate the self-worth and net-worth of women around the world."*

MELODY THOMPSON

Randall S. Hansen, Ph.D., Founder of Quintessential Careers: *"To make a difference in people's lives through expert advice, personal empowerment, and compassion."*

Makeda Pennycooke, Women's Empowerment Coach: *"Through faith, vulnerability and an anchoring presence, I hold space for others to courageously risk revealing their messy, broken pieces; discover the redemptive power of grace, and stand in their most authentic truth so they may unravel into their best selves."*

PROSPER ON PURPOSE

Developing Your Mission Statement

Use the following questions to develop your mission statement.

Mission Statement Questions

1. What are my top three strengths, gifts and talents I utilize in my work?

2. How do I provide my gifts and talents? What methods do I use to offer my gifts and talents?

3. Who do I want to help (my audience)?

4. What issues do they have?

5. How do I help my audience? What do I enable them to do?

6. What makes me unique?

7. What are my top five core values that relate to my work?

PROSPER ON PURPOSE

Mission Statement Sentence Outlines

Below are four templates to use to create a mission statement. Fill in the blanks, using your answers from the previous questions, to develop a mission statement sentence. This is only a guideline. Feel free to write your own mission statement in your own words.

1 My mission is to use my gifts of _____,
(strength)

_____ and _____ to
(strength) (strength)

_____ and _____ for
(unique solution) (unique solution)

_____.
(your audience)

2 My mission is to _____ for
(unique solution)

_____ through
(your audience)

_____, _____
(method) (method)

and _____.
(method)

MELODY THOMPSON

3) Through _____, _____
            (method)   (method)

and _____ I provide
      (method)

_____ for _____
(unique solution)   (your audience)

to _____. I provide
   (do these specific tasks)

_____ to meet their needs, in a way that is
(unique solution)

_____, _____ and
(your values)   (your values)

_____.
(your values)

4) Using _____, I provide
        (method)

_____ for _____.
(unique solution)   (your audience)

I provide my services to address the unique needs of

_____ who _____.
(your audience)   (have this issue)

I provide _____ to meet
        (unique solution)

their needs, in a way that is _____.
                      (your values)

PROSPER ON PURPOSE

Mission Statement Questions - Sample

Below is an example of answers to the mission statement questions.

1. What are my top three strengths, gifts and talents I utilize in my work?

    Teaching, Communication and Compassion

2. What methods do I use to offer my gifts and talents?

    Training, Coaching & Consulting

3. Who do I want to help? Who is my audience/my target market?

    Entrepreneurs

4. What issues do they have?

    May not have prior business experience, may be lacking support, may need mentorship, coaching and training.

5. How do I help my audience/my target market?

   Provide resources to help them start, grow and maintain a successful small business.

6. What makes me unique?

   I provide coaching and training to small business owners that need business skills and who want to develop their own marketing strategy.

7. What are my top three core values that relate to my work?

   Encouragement, Empowerment, Education

Sample Mission Statement (using answers)

Below is a sample mission statement that was developed using the answers to the previous questions.

Using *training, coaching and consulting programs*, I provide *entrepreneurial support* for *starting, growing and maintaining a successful small business*. I customize my products and services to address the unique needs of *female entrepreneurs* who *may have no prior business experience, no support and no access to business education or mentors*. I provide *training, support and coaching* to meet their needs, in a way that is *encouraging, empowering and educational*.

Write Your Mission Statement

Using the answers to the previous questions, write your mission statement below.

Purpose Plan

Now we will begin to put together the pieces of the puzzle. On the next page, you will begin putting together your Purpose Plan. You will fill in the answers to the questions you've answered in previous chapters, to develop a complete purpose plan.

You will answer questions on your passions, values, mission and power. This will help you formulate a more complete picture of who you are, why you do what you do and where you are going.

Purpose Plan

Theme

What is the word that best describes your focus for the next year?

Mission Statement

What is your mission/purpose statement?

Vision Statement

What is your vision statement?

Slogan/Motto

What are your top 2 favorite life mottos or quotes that best reflect your values or viewpoint on life?

Personality

What are the top 3 "I AM" identity statements that best describe you?

What are the top 3 words that describe your personal brand identity?

What are your top 2 intelligences?

What is your preferred learning or working style?

What are your top 3 strengths?

What are 3 things that make you unique?

What are 3 ways you plan to improve in the next year?

If you could choose one word to describe yourself, what would it be?

MELODY THOMPSON

Perspective

What are 3 things you will tell yourself when you feel afraid, unworthy or incapable?

Name three ways your perspective changed in the past 2 weeks.

What do you believe about yourself now that you didn't believe when you started this book?

Passions

What are your top 5 passions?

What are your top 5 core values?

Legacy – What are the top 5 things you want to be known for?

Position

What are some of your past successes?

What positions have prepared you for your purpose?

What have the positions you've held in life taught you?

What are the top 5 goals of things you want to do in the future?

What are the top 5 goals of who you want to be in the future?

What are the top 5 goals of what you want to have in the future?

What are your top 5 Wheel of Life Goals for the next year?

Power

What top 5 empowerment rights resonate the most with you?

Name 5 ways you will tap into your personal power.

PROSPER ON PURPOSE

What is your new perspective on fear? On Failure?

What 5 things you will cut off that no longer serve you?

What 5 things will you add to your life that will empower you?

What are 3 ways you will fill your own cup?

Purpose

Where do your strengths, passions and values align?

What is the common theme in your strengths, passions and values?

What do you believe is your assignment?

What is your announcement?

Who is your audience?

How do you help others?

What adjustments are you willing to make in your life in order to reach your purpose?

CONCLUSION

Congratulations! You have worked through the steps of discovering more about your identity, what thoughts may be holding you back, how to tap into your passions, what important positions you've held in your life, how to walk in your personal power and how to define your purpose.

At this point, you understand how your identity is closely tied to your purpose. I hope the exercises and questions helped you understand more about your gifts, talents and skills along with what types of intelligence you possess. It is so important to discover who you are and live authentically. When you know your identity, it becomes the ticket to gain access to places in life that are looking for exactly who you are and what you have to offer.

Examining your perspective can help you dig deeper into the thoughts that motivate you as well as ones that may have held you back in the past. When we explore our beliefs and mindsets, we can take control of how our thoughts affect us in our careers and relationships. We can remove labels and mindsets that don't serve us, allowing us to discover the truth about our potential. This is the beginning of living in freedom.

Hopefully, you were able to use the self reflection questions to uncover some of your passions. Sometimes our passions can been buried under all of our day to day responsibilities, however we can rediscover them by spending time focusing on what makes us happy. Not all of our passions will be able to serve others or generate income. While some of our passions may lead us to our purpose or serve as a way to make additional income, it is fine to have passions that serve no other purpose than to bring us joy and reduce stress in our lives.

Taking a look at the places we've been in our lives and the unique experiences we've had, whether good or bad, can help us define where we are going. We've all had stops on our journey of life and each place provides us with some information that can be used in another part of our life if we take the time to evaluate our experiences and learn the lessons from them.

Knowing that your time and energy are valuable helps to ensure you spend it wisely. Having healthy boundaries allows us to manage how we allocate our time and where we spend our energy. We can politely decline requests that are not in alignment with our purpose or our personal values. When we become empowered to take accountability for our lives, we can in turn empower others.

Defining your purpose is not a one time event. It is a lifelong process. I believe we as human beings are multifaceted, ever evolving and always becoming a greater version of our true selves every day. If you are still searching for your purpose, just know it will happen at the right time. We cannot rush the process of purpose. Remember, you are always serving a purpose at every stage of your life. Even if you don't feel significant right now, you *are*. Someone needs you, even if you haven't met them yet. So, keep learning, growing, studying and preparing because your time will come. When it does, you'll be ready.

I just want to leave you with my well wishes for you: May you find the purpose for which you were created and pursue it passionately. May you find significance, balance, fulfillment and prosperity in everything you do. May you have everything you need to succeed. May you do everything in love and treat everyone you meet with kindness. May your hope never fail and your joy never cease. Wishing you all the best on your journey!

SOURCES

Duhigg, Charles and Chamberlain, Mike (2012). The Power of Habit. New York, N.Y.: Random House.

Dweck, C. S., & Joosr. (2015). Mindset by Carol Dweck: The new psychology of success. Clitheroe, United Kingdom: Joosr.

Gardner, Howard (1983), Frames of Mind: The Theory of Multiple Intelligences

Mcgraw, Phil (2013). Life Code: The New Rules for Winning in the Real World. Ingram Pub Services.

Made in the USA
Monee, IL
07 February 2021